Ray Pritchard is a man who believes and lives his faith and is a practitioner of what he believes. If you desire to strengthen and deepen your faith in every season of life and develop a muscular faith, then read Keep Believing. Here you will find honest and helpful answers to life's questions and discover a faith for a lifetime. I absolutely love this book and you will too!

Dr. Jack Graham
Prestonwood Baptist Church, Plano, TX
Author of *Unseen, Angels, Marriage by the Book*
Speaker on PowerPoint TV and radio ministry

Keep Believing will help anyone trying to find God when life tumbles in. This book offers biblical answers to the hard questions that keep us awake at night. Pastor Ray enables us to keep on keeping on we feel like giving up. Read it! Study it! Share it with a friend!

H.B. Charles, Jr.
Pastor, Shiloh Metropolitan Baptist Church
Jacksonville, FL
Author of *It Happens After Prayer*

Dr. Ray Pritchard offers hope for the hurting based on the eternal truth of God's Word. I recommend this book to anyone going through hard times because it will give you hope to keep on believing when you'd rather give up.

Bobby Richardson
Former New York Yankee
All-Star Second Baseman
World Series MVP

Winston Churchill famously said: "If you are going through hell, keep going." In this wonderful book Ray Pritchard gives us biblical reasons to keep believing during the hard times, reasons that will fuel our ability to keep going until the better times.

Philip De Courcy
Pastor of Kindred Community Church
Anaheim Hills, California
Teacher on the daily radio broadcast Know the Truth.

Read this book now, even if you're not presently hurting, because it will help prepare you to keep believing when the tough times come—and they will. This book helped me to realize that many of my "why" questions are never meant to be answered. The real question becomes, "Am I going to keep believing even though I don't understand?"

Brian Bill
Pastor, Edgewood Baptist Church
Rock Island, IL
Speaker, "On Mission" radio broadcast

Keep Believing is A learning tool for the mature Christian, and for the person searching for peace when the bottom drops out and life is hard to take. Once I started reading it, I couldn't put it down! I highly recommend it! This book belongs on the top shelf of your library. Outstanding!

Thomas S. Klobucher
Founder and CEO Thomas Interiors Inc.
Author of eight books in the *Lifetime Learning* Series

Keep Believing is written for all of us who struggle with "the stuff" that life is made of. For those who question, there are biblical answers. For those who doubt, there is assurance. For those who get discouraged, there is encouragement. And for those who lose focus, there is direction.

Tom Phillips
Campus Pastor
Word of Life Bible Institute
Pottersville, NY

In Keep Believing, Dr. Pritchard presents men and women of faith and their questions and struggles. These are juxtaposed with scriptural principles that shed light and understanding on God, who "causes all things to work together for good." Keep Believing will provide insight to help you strengthen your faith when life is rough.

Dr. Tom Renard
Pediatric Surgeon
Dallas, Texas

This insightful work, borne from experience, expertly encourages Christians toward faith first in our search for peace amid life's inevitable struggles. In Keep Believing, my longtime friend Ray Pritchard shares beautifully and creatively scriptural solutions to life's struggles. His qualifications are validated by his experiences. This is an inspiring and fresh look at the awesome truth of God's Sovereignty!

Rev. Ron Lambe
Baton Rouge, Louisiana

KEEP

FINDING GOD IN YOUR
DEEPEST STRUGGLES

BELIEVING

RAY PRITCHARD

Cover design and interior layout by Josh Pritchard

GIDEON HOUSE BOOKS

www.gideonhousebooks.com

Printed in the USA
Signature Book Printing, www.sbpbooks.com

In memory of my father

and my mother

from a very grateful son

CONTENTS

ACKNOWLEDGEMENTS

When I wrote the first edition of this book in 1996, I noted the help I had received from Greg Thornton, Jim Bell, and Julie Ieron along with several others from Moody Publishers. Lisa King gave great encouragement along the way. Brian Bill offered wise counsel. I mentioned that the first edition was written during some trying times in my own life, and I thanked our three sons and my wife. Looking back, I dimly remember those trying times, but I will never forget how Marlene and our three sons supported me.

For this second edition, my gratitude to Marlene is even greater because she has shouldered extra burdens while I have recovered from my biking accident. But without that accident, this new edition would not happen. I am grateful to the board of Keep Believing Ministries for their love and their prayers and their continual support. Special thanks to Josh Pritchard for designing the cover and putting the book in print through Gideon House.

FOREWORD

I have been waiting for someone to write this book! And I already have a list of people who need its message now! Every writer has a target audience in mind, defined either by age, class, or specific need. This book encompasses virtually everyone. Those who are facing tragedies will find it comforting; those whose lives are momentarily free from tears will be better prepared to help others who are struggling with the harsh realities of life.

Pastor Pritchard takes the promises of God in one hand and the anguishing questions of life in the other and brings them together, convinced that the Bible has something to say to us when life tumbles in. You will get the feeling that you are eavesdropping, listening in as he pours salve on fresh wounds of sorrow, comforting those who find their faith sliding on the slope of a question mark.

What makes this book special is its compelling realism. Every reader will be persuaded that Pastor Pritchard has indeed heard all of us. He has sat with us in a hospital waiting room, hearing the news that a child has died; he has listened to a man grieve over the death of his marriage. He knows the keen disappointment of unanswered prayer. He knows that we cannot comfort others by trying to minimize the pain of loneliness and personal anguish. He does not preach at us but takes us by the hand and leads us back to where we need to be.

This book has added credibility because the author does not pretend to have all the answers. Rather, he points us to God and

3

reminds us that we have nowhere else to go. With God there are few answers; without God there are none. So in the presence of the Almighty, we do not have all of our questions answered, but we do find help and comfort. On our knees we will come to agree with the man who said, "As Christians we live by promises, not explanations."

Finally, readers will appreciate Pastor Pritchard's writing style. He not only communicates information but paints pictures, so that we can identify with the issues discussed. I found myself saying, "Yes ... I've felt that way ... and those are the questions that have often plagued my mind."

Read it! Study it! Share it!

Dr. Erwin W. Lutzer
Pastor Emeritus
The Moody Church
Chicago, IL

INTRODUCTION

Everyone has a story to tell, even the people who seem to smile all the time. This is one of the first things a young pastor learns when he graduates from seminary and begins his ministry. Some people look so well-adjusted and happy that you think they don't have a care in the world. But they do. If you work with people long enough, you discover that even the "perfect" people know all about sorrow and heartache.

If you stay in one church long enough, you begin to hear the stories. Everybody has one. A tale of sadness or of failure. A story of a broken marriage, a child with an incurable disease, alcohol abuse, crushing financial disaster, loved ones far from God, and dreams dashed on the jagged rocks of reality. Every face has its own secret story. The pastor soon learns to look behind the smile for the shadows that are always there. Sometimes it takes a while, and sometimes he hears about it second- or third-hand, but over time, the truth comes out and the story is told. But the pastor is not surprised, for behind his own smiling face are many stories, some so painful they are never told, others only alluded to here and there, little whispers of past difficulties that the discerning listener hears even if he doesn't fully understand.

This book is addressed to those people who want to know what God has to say about their pain, their sadness, their failures, and their unanswered prayers. Many of them have secretly given up on God because they feel he has wounded them and can no longer be trusted. Others grimly hold on to faith because they have nowhere else to turn.

To all those people, God says, "I am still here, and I care about you." The chapters of this book reinforce that truth by bringing the reader face-to-face with God. Some of the chapters sketch out the problems of life, some tackle difficult theological issues, and still others revisit well-known biblical texts that call us to a higher view of God and a deep trust in our Creator. One chapter was born on a hot summer afternoon in Southern California during a doctoral seminar when Vernon Grounds gave the first explanation of Romans 8:28 that made sense to me. The chapter on doubt came from a message I gave at Moody Founder's Week in Chicago. I included a chapter on "Praying for your Prodigal" because almost everyone has a prodigal among their family and friends.

When I wrote the first edition of this book, I was in my mid-40s. Back then Marlene and I were raising our three growing boys in the Chicago suburb of Oak Park where I served as pastor of Calvary Memorial Church. Fast forward 20 years and I am now past retirement age, our boys have grown up and gotten married, Marlene and I are grandparents, and our family is scattered across America. For the last thirteen years, we have served with Keep Believing Ministries.

For those who may wonder, the book came first, the ministry much later. The name didn't originate with me. When I turned in the manuscript, I called it something else, but the good folks at Moody Publishing suggested *Keep Believing*, and the name stuck and eventually became the name of our ministry. If I have any special qualification for what I am doing now, it would be that I have often found it hard to keep believing. What I'm writing about is not theoretical in any case. These pages contain the questions I have wrestled with and the answers that satisfy my soul.

On a purely personal note, I intended to publish this new edition of Keep Believing a few years ago, but other projects kept getting in the way. Then in early January 2019, I slipped on the ice while riding my bike. I ended up breaking three bones in my left leg and dislocating my ankle. After three surgeries and a long rehab, I'm getting better slowly.

This isn't something I would have chosen, but I know my accident was just an "incident" in God's plan. By taking me off my feet, the Lord gave me time to work on this project.

God knows how to change our plans, doesn't he?

I'm glad about it because this down time has allowed me to go back and think through what I wrote over 20 years ago. Time has strengthened my conviction that God is good and can be trusted in every situation.

The biggest barrier to faith is life itself. More than once I have been asked "Why?" only to shake my head in wonderment at the strange acts of God. I cannot explain why a good man dies at 42, leaving behind a wife and four children. But my friend died as a Christian, still believing in God to the very end. I have seen that happen often enough to know that the Christian faith provides answers that cannot be found anywhere else.

I have spent hours pondering these questions with friends who cling to faith as their last resort. Needless to say, these chapters are not the last word on the subject of suffering and the Christian faith. They represent the things I have learned by spending time with the people of God in some difficult moments. When you have finished this book, you will still have many questions, but I hope you will be encouraged to keep on believing in God.

1

WHEN LIFE TUMBLES IN, WHAT THEN?

When his wife died, he didn't know at first how he would survive. Although he was a minister and had helped many others through times of crisis, now he faced his own personal moment of truth. How would he reconcile his own loss with the Christian faith he claimed to believe? What would he say to his own grieving congregation?

The year was 1927. The place: Aberdeen, Scotland. The man: Arthur John Gossip, pastor of the Beechgrove Church. He was 54 years old and at the height of his powers.

Historians tell us he was humble and sincere, possessing a keen wit and deeply devoted to his family and friends. A bit of an eccentric, he sometimes scandalized his staid Scottish congregation by appearing in public with a floppy fisherman's hat perched on his head. He was a man of strong opinions who never held back from expressing them to any and all who cared to listen. History also tells us he was beloved as a pastor and preacher.

In fact, he is remembered as a preacher primarily for one particular sermon he preached in 1927. Widely regarded as one of the greatest ever preached, it was the first sermon he delivered after the sudden death of his wife. He titled his message "But When Life Tumbles In, What Then?" In it, he struggled to reconcile his Christian faith with the loss of a loved one.

These are his words:

> I do not understand this life of ours. But still less can I comprehend how people in trouble and loss and bereavement can fling away peevishly from the Christian faith. In God's name, fling to what? Have we not lost enough without losing that too?

How right he was. "So many people's religion is a fair-weather affair," as he put it. "A little rain, and it runs and crumbles; a touch of strain, and it snaps." But if we turn from faith in the time of trouble, what shall we turn to? Have we not lost enough without losing that too?

Let us begin our journey together by spending some time in the book of Job. That is not the only place we could begin, but it makes sense to start there, because Job deals with timeless questions of suffering and loss. Even though the story is 4000 years old, it could have been written yesterday. Most of the book of Job is poetry, and the book has been called the greatest poem in all human history. One writer noted that "it bears the stamp of uncommon genius."

The book abounds with mysteries: Who wrote it? When? Where? Why? But the greatest mystery is found in the subject matter itself: the mystery of undeserved suffering. Why do bad things happen to good people? For centuries, thoughtful readers have pondered that question. Why do babies die? Why are innocent people held hostage by madmen? Why are the righteous passed over for promotion while the wicked cheat and lie their way to the top?

The book does not answer those questions with a theory. It answers them with a story. We are invited to examine one man whose life tumbled in around him. Why did that happen and what did he do about it?

The Man Who Had It All

The book of Job has a terse beginning. Job 1 unfolds likes film running at hyperspeed. The frames zip by one after the other as an entire life is squeezed into a handful of sentences.

The first five verses tell us three things about Job.

He Was a Righteous Man

"In the land of Uz there lived a man whose name was Job. This man was blameless and upright; he feared God and shunned evil" (Job 1:1). You could talk for hours about those four phrases: blameless, upright, fearing God, shunning evil. But suffice it to say that Job was as good a man as you will find in all the Bible.

He Was a Rich Man

"He had seven sons and three daughters, and he owned seven thousand sheep, three thousand camels, five hundred yoke of oxen and five hundred donkeys, and had a large number of servants. He was the greatest man among all the people of the East" (vv. 2–3).

It is hard to know how to translate this sentence into today's terms. I thought of Warren Buffet or Mark Zuckerberg or Bill Gates, but they don't fit the image. Maybe I could say it this way. The richest man in the world is currently worth $108 billion. By spelling out the details about the sheep and camels and oxen and donkeys, our text is telling us that if a list of the world's richest people had been printed 4000 years ago, Job would have been at the top.

He Was a Religious Man

"His sons used to take turns holding feasts in their homes, and they would invite their three sisters to eat and drink with them. When a period of feasting had run its course, Job would send and have them purified. Early in the morning he would sacrifice a burnt offering for each of them, thinking, 'Perhaps my children have sinned and cursed God in their hearts.' This was Job's regular custom" (vv. 4–5). Here is that rarest of all rare creatures: A truly wealthy man who loves God more than he loves his money. Not only that, but here is a father who takes responsibility for the spiritual welfare of his own family.

The point of these first few verses is very clear: By the world's standards, Job was successful; by God's standards, he was righteous. *Here is a man who truly had it all.* He was wealthy and godly and popular. You couldn't find a person who would say a bad word about Job. I repeat what I said earlier—he is as good a man as you will find in all the Bible.

That fact is crucial to understanding his story. Let me say it carefully. What happened to him happened because he was a good man! Nothing in the book of Job makes sense unless that is true. Job offers us a case study in the suffering of the righteous. As hard as it may be to understand, it was his righteousness and his prosperity that brought about his enormous suffering. And yet the suffering was undeserved in the truest sense of the word.

Enter Satan

While you ponder that, consider what happens next. The story suddenly shifts to Job's first test. The scene changes from earth to heaven. Job apparently never knew about this part of the story. While he was on the earth tending to his vast holdings, Satan was having a conversation with God:

> One day the angels [the Hebrew calls them "the sons of God"] came to present themselves before the Lord, and Satan [the name means "accuser," and Satan will now live up to his name] also came with them. The Lord said to Satan, 'Where have you come from?'

Satan answered the Lord, 'From roaming through the earth and going back and forth in it' (vv. 6–7).

This passage corrects a prevailing misconception about Satan. If you ask the average Christian, "Where is Satan today?" most will say that Satan is in hell. But the Bible does not teach that. If Satan were in hell today, we would have no problems at all. As one writer puts it, "Satan is alive and well on planet earth." In this age the earth is under his power and domination. Thank God, the day will come when Satan and all his hordes will be cast into the lake of fire forever (Matthew 25:41; Revelation 20:10). But that won't happen until Jesus returns to the earth. Between now and then, Satan roams about on the earth like a roaring lion, seeking men and women he can devour (1 Peter 5:8).

The Bible teaches there is a personal being called Satan who, though once an angel of God, rebelled and fell from heaven to earth. In that rebellion he led one-third of the angels with him. Those fallen angels became the demons. From the day of his fall until now, Satan has had but one purpose: to frustrate God's plan by seeking to destroy men and women on the earth. After all these thousands of years, he is still at it.

Satan was behind what happened to Job. Job never knew that and God never told him, but the writer of the book lets us peek behind the heavenly curtain to see the unfolding drama.

Satan Is Not the Issue

That brings us to the key passage. Notice in verse 8 that it is God who brings Job's name up. "Have you considered my servant Job? There is no one on earth like him." That's the other side of the coin. Satan was behind Job's trials, but God was behind Satan. It's not Satan who brings Job up. It's God.

It is as if God were saying, "All right, Satan, you're looking for a good man. Let me tell you about Job. He's the best man I've got. I don't think you can break him down."

What an insight that is.

Behind the suffering is Satan, and behind Satan is God. That is why, as you read the book of Job, you find that Job is complaining against God. He never brings up Satan because Satan is not the issue; God is.

Even though Satan was the one who caused the calamity, he did so with God's permission. If God had not given his permission, Satan could not have touched a hair of Job's head.

Does Job Serve God for Nothing?

In verse 9 we come to the key question of the book: "Does Job fear God for nothing?" Satan is accusing God of bribing Job into worshiping him. After all, Job has it all: a huge, loving family, enormous wealth, a great reputation—everything in this world a man could want. No wonder he worships God. Who wouldn't?

That's what Satan means when he says in verse 10, "Have you not put a hedge around him?" He means something like this: "You gave him all of that and then you protect him from anything that could harm him. He's living on easy street; he doesn't have a worry in the world. No wonder he's your best man. He's also your richest man. You take care of your own, don't you?"

Behind it all is a not-so-subtle message. You've bribed him with prosperity. You dangle riches in front of him like a carrot on a stick. *Satan is accusing God of rigging the system.* It's as if God and Job had a contract that went like this:

I'll be good, and you will bless me.
I'll be pious, and you will give me prosperity.

This is the Old Testament version of what today is called Prosperity Theology. Note that it comes from Satan, not from God. Satan is attacking Job's motive and God's integrity. Here is the real question of the book of Job: Will anyone serve God for no personal gain?

Satan says the answer is no. Job will worship God only when things are going his way. Thus he says in verse 11: "But stretch out your hand and strike everything he has, and he will surely curse you to your face."

Satan's question is the supreme question of life. You served God in the sunshine; will you now serve him in the shadows? You believed him in the light of day; will you still believe him at midnight? You sang his praises when all was going well; will you still sing through your tears? You came to church and declared, "The Lord is my Shepherd. I shall not want." Is he still your shepherd in the valley of the shadow of death?

He was good enough for you when you had money in the bank. Is he good enough for you when you have no money at all? He was good enough for you when you had your health. Is he good enough when the doctor says, "You have six months to live"? He was good enough when you were married. Is he good enough when your spouse walks out on you? He was good enough when your family was all together. Is he good enough when you stand around an open grave?

It's not hard to believe in God when everything is going your way. Anyone can do that. But when life tumbles in, what then?

Four Messengers of Misfortune

Now the scene shifts from heaven to earth. Satan has received God's permission to put Job to the test. It happens on a "day when Job's sons and daughters were feasting and drinking wine at the oldest brother's house" (v. 13). In a moment of great happiness, at a family reunion, when you would least expect it, Satan strikes.

First, the Sabeans steal Job's livestock and kill his servants (vv. 14–15). *Second*, a "fire of God" destroys his sheep and kills his servants (v. 16). *Third*, the Chaldeans steal his camels and kill his servants (v. 17). *Fourth*, a great wind hits the house where his children are feasting and kills them all (vv. 18–19).

The four messengers of misfortune come to Job one after another. Three times the text says, "While he was still speaking" (vv. 16, 17, 18). In the space of a few minutes, Job lost everything that was dear to him. His vast wealth: vanished. His empire: crumbled. His workers: murdered. His children: killed.

That's the worst of it. When tragedy strikes, it often comes again and again. And we think, "This must be the worst of it." Then comes another knock at the door. Just when it seems that things can't get any more terrible, the bottom falls out again.

370 and Rising

Have you ever taken one of those tests designed to measure the stress in your life? Typically, the test lists 50 stress-producing events and assigns a numerical score to each event.

Some events have a relatively low point value:

Moving to a new home: 20 points
Trouble with in-laws: 29 points

Others produce much more stress:

Divorce: 73 points
Death of a spouse: 100 points

You simply check off the events that have happened to you in the last 12 months and then total up the points. According to the test, if your total score for a year is from 0 to 150, you have only a 37 percent chance of undergoing a severe mental or emotional crisis in the next two years. If your score is from 150 to 300, the probability rises to 51 percent. But if your score is over 300, there is an 80 percent probability that you will soon face a severe mental or emotional crisis. The stress level in your life is simply too high.

Something like that happened to me in 1974. That was the year the bottom fell out of my life. In less than six months I got engaged, graduated from college, took a new job, went on a long trip, got married, moved to a new state, started seminary, and two months later my father died. My score on the stress scale was up to 370 and rising.

By the end of the year I was a basket case. Everything good was bitter to me. I hated life. It had been too much to take.

But Job lost it all, not in a year or in six months or in a couple of weeks, but in a single afternoon. *Tragedy is no respecter of persons.* You can be on top of the world and lose it all in the twinkling of an eye. Tragedy can come to the same house again and again, and there is nothing we can do to stop it.

From Weeping to Worship

The only thing that is left is to see Job's response.
There Is Genuine Sorrow.

"At this, Job got up and tore his robe and shaved his head" (v. 20). These are the actions of a man whose heart has been torn apart. They are public symbols of inner pain, much like wearing black to a funeral.

Some Christians think it is wrong to grieve over a great loss. They believe tears somehow show a lack of faith in God. Even in a great loss, they believe it is somehow holy to put up a good front and never show pain. They even have trouble dealing with people who show great emotion after a severe loss.

I remember discussing this with a friend who told me that when his father died, he never cried, not even once. He simply called the undertaker, and that was that. When I told him I had cried many times in thinking about my father's death, he simply could not understand it. To him, tears were a sign of weakness. But the Bible never says that. We are told that "Jesus wept" (John 11:35). Abraham and David and Jeremiah were real flesh-and-blood men who were not afraid to weep and cry and cover themselves with mourning garments. No one believed in God more than they did, and yet they were not ashamed to let others see their pain.

We do not have a high priest who cannot be touched with our weaknesses (see Hebrews 4:15). Jesus knows what we're going through because he was here with us. He knows what it's like to die of a broken heart. If our Lord was not ashamed of his tears, we shouldn't be ashamed of ours.

There Is Heartfelt Worship.

"Then he fell to the ground in worship" (Job 1:20). Here is the ultimate response of the man of faith in the face of unexplainable tragedy. He weeps and then he worships. This is what differentiates the Christian from the rest of the world. They weep; we weep. They get angry; we worship. Our sorrow is just as real as theirs, but their sorrow leads only to despair, whereas ours leads to worship.

There Is Profound Faith.

Verse 21 records Job's great statement of faith. He says three things.

"Naked I came from my mother's womb, and naked I will depart."

All babies are born naked. We have a phrase for that. We say that a naked person is wearing his "birthday suit." But it's just as true at the end of life. We leave the way we enter. We bring nothing with us, and we take nothing with us. Sometimes when a person dies, we ask, "How much did he leave?" The answer is always the same: "He left it all." An Italian proverb says, "The last robe has no pockets." You'll never see a Brink's truck following a hearse. When you die, you leave it all behind.

All we have is given to us as a temporary loan. No matter how much we have been given in this life, we cannot keep it. In the end we must give it back.

"The Lord gave and the Lord has taken away."

This is the man of faith speaking. This statement rises above the first one. It is true that we leave it all behind. But the man of faith understands that all we have we never owned in the first place. All that we have was given to us by God. He can take what is rightfully his anytime he wants. Because he is God, he doesn't have to ask our permission before he takes it back, nor does he have to explain himself afterward.

"May the name of the Lord be praised."

Job's faith now rises to its highest level. He has lost it all: his wealth, his workers, his children. All that he counted dear in life has been ripped from his grasp. Yet in the midst of his pain, Job praises God.

Here is the great point: Job draws his argument for praise from the bitterness of suffering. His loss drives him back to the goodness of God. Every pain is a reminder of how good God has been to him.

Someone has said that "the magnitude of the loss determines the size of the gift." The greater the sorrow, the greater the joy must have been. Every tear is a way of saying, "Thank you, Lord, for what you gave me." In Job's case, the more he grieves, the more he blesses the name of the Lord.

Four Simple Conclusions

Our text ends with these amazing words: "In all this, Job did not sin by charging God with wrongdoing" (v. 22). He didn't ask why, he didn't accuse God of not loving him, he didn't claim his rights, he didn't curse God, and he didn't give up his faith. He simply said to himself, "If God takes something away from me, I will thank him that I had it to enjoy for a little while."

As I ponder this remarkable story, four conclusions come to mind.

1. Undeserved suffering often comes to righteous men and women.

This is surely an obvious lesson, and although we have heard it before, we need to hear it again. Three times the text emphasizes that Job was a righteous man. His suffering did not happen because of any moral fault or hidden sin in his life. It is a human tendency when tragedy strikes to believe that if we had only lived a better life, the tragedy would never have happened. Sometimes that is true, but more often it is not. If the story of Job teaches us anything, it is that godly people sometimes suffer unexplainable losses. Terrible things sometimes happen to God's people.

2. God is the source and owner of all you have.

God is the ultimate source of all you have, and he has the absolute right to take that which belongs to him. Your house? It is his. Your job? It is his. Your future? It is his. Your health? It is his. Your children? Yes, even your children are his. They belonged to him before they ever belonged to you. Your husband or your wife? Yes, even your husband or your wife. All you have belongs to God. And in the end, you will give it all back to him. Sometimes he will take back something sooner than you would like to give it. But that is his absolute right, for he is God.

3. Your trials relate to God's purpose for your life.

Your trials can never be caused by blind fate or bad luck. They all somehow relate to God's purpose for your life. If this were not true, the Bible would not be true. If you don't come to believe this, you will eventually give up your faith. When tragedy strikes, we want to search for a cause, a reason, an explanation, a chain of events stretching back into the past that would explain the catastrophe you now face. But as you search for causes, you will go back, and back, and back, until at last you come to God. If you do not eventually conclude that what happens to you somehow flows from God's loving purpose for your life, you will sooner or later give up your faith altogether.

4. Your trials are designed to draw you nearer to God.

When tragedy strikes, we want to know, "Why did this happen to me?" The deeper question is, "Now that this has happened, will I remain loyal to God?"

That brings us back to A. J. Gossip's sermon and the great question, "When life tumbles in, what then?" If we turn away from our faith in times of trouble, what shall we turn to? Have we not lost enough without losing that too? When life crashes in against us and all we value most is taken from us, if we then give up our faith, where will we go and what will we do?

Pastor Gossip puts it this way in his sermon:

> You people in the sunshine may believe the faith, but we in the shadow must believe it. We have nothing else.

Steve Brown tells about a seminar one of his associate pastors was leading. During one session, the associate pastor said that because God is love, no matter how bad things get, Christians should praise him. Afterward, a man came up to him in great agitation. "Dave, I can't buy it. I can't buy what you say about praising God during evil and hurt." Then he went on to say what many people secretly feel. "I do not believe that when you lose someone you love through death, or you have cancer, or you lose your job, that you ought to praise God." After a moment's silence, the associate pastor replied very simply, "What alternative do you propose?"

We do not gain if we turn away from God in the time of trouble. If we turn away from God, we lose our only ground of hope.

Cords Stronger Than Steel

As A. J. Gossip came to the end of his sermon, he said,

> I don't think you need to be afraid of life. Our hearts are very frail; and there are places where the road is very steep and very lonely. But we have a wonderful God.

Indeed we do. And as the apostle Paul puts it at the end of Romans 8, What can separate us from the love of God? Nothing at all. Not life, nor death, nor tragedy, nor heartbreak, nor suffering. We are forever connected to his love with cords a thousand times stronger than steel. Nothing can separate us from the love of God that is in Christ Jesus our Lord.

The question remains. When life tumbles in, what then? Through our tears, we rest our confidence in one great truth. He who has led us this far on our journey will take us safely home.

2

THE BLESSING NO ONE WANTS

"Blessed are those who mourn, for they will be comforted"
(Matthew 5:4).

This is one of the strangest statements in the Bible. *It is a paradox and a mystery.* "Blessed are those who mourn," said Jesus. Happy are the sad! What do these strange words mean? Who are the mourners, why are they sad, and how are they comforted?

The Mystery of Human Suffering

Most of us know about Jim Elliot, the missionary martyr who died in Ecuador in January 1956 when he and four other missionaries were killed by the Auca Indians (now called the Waoranis). The story made headlines around the world and inspired books, films, and generations of Christian missionaries. His wife, Elizabeth, told the story in several books, including the bestselling *Through Gates of Splendor*. More than a half-century later, we still repeat Jim Elliot's famous words, "He is no fool who gives what he cannot keep to gain that which he cannot lose."

Jim Elliot's story gripped the evangelical world, making him arguably the most famous missionary of the 20thcentury. What most people don't know is that he had an older brother who went to Peru as a missionary in 1949. During his 62 years on the field, Bert Elliot established 150 churches. He died in Trujillo, Peru, on February 17, 2012, at the age of 87. When Randy Alcorn interviewed him in 2006, Bert described his younger brother this way:

> Jim and I both served Christ, but differently. He was a great meteor, streaking through the sky.

Bert Elliot was home on furlough when Jim and the other missionaries were killed. He and his wife wrestled with whether or not they should return to the field:

> "Why doesn't God take care of us?" he remembered asking. "If we give our lives to serve him, how come there's not the protection?" The answer that came to him then became the hallmark of his own life. "It's in dying that we're born to eternal life," he said. "It's not maintaining our lives, but it's giving our lives." So a few months later, Bert Elliot and his wife Colleen returned to the jungles of Peru (Life story on OregonLive.com).

Randy Alcorn described Bert Elliot as a "faint star that rose night after night, faithfully crossing the same path in the sky, to God's glory."

Jim Elliot was a great meteor, streaking through the sky.
Bert Elliot was a faint star, crossing the same path night after night.

Which one did the greater work?
Why did one die young and the other live 87 years?

No matter how long we ponder the matter, these questions cannot easily be answered because "the secret things belong to the Lord our God" (Deuteronomy 29:29). *God has his reasons, but he's not obligated to explain them to us.* The "secret things" describe the deep purposes of God that we simply are not capable of understanding. What sort of explanation would suffice to explain to us why one man lives while another man dies?

Strange Pain

I still remember the last time I saw Peter Blakemore. It happened at a pastor's prayer meeting in connection with the National Day of Prayer. I came a few minutes late and found the men gathered in a circle ready to pray. As I walked in, I recognized most of the pastors immediately, except for one man in a wheelchair who was facing away from me. He had two teenage boys by his side.

When I sat down, I realized the man in the wheelchair was Peter Blakemore, pastor of Harrison Street Bible Church in Oak Park, Illinois. Peter was 42 years old, married, with seven children. He had lived in Oak Park all his life, the only exception being the years he spent in college and graduate school. His father pastored Harrison Street Bible Church for over 30 years, and then Peter took up the ministry in his father's stead.

It all started when Peter noticed a strange pain that wouldn't go away. He sought medical help, but the doctors couldn't pinpoint the source of trouble. Eventually they found a tumor, performed a biopsy, and sent it off for analysis. It took a long time to get a correct answer, but in due course a lab on the West Coast reported that Peter had contracted a rare form of cancer. He began chemotherapy in a desperate attempt to eradicate it.

When I saw Peter at the prayer meeting, he was bent over a bit, but smiling as he sat in the wheelchair. As we prayed, I heard a strange noise coming from my left. It was Peter's eldest son, rubbing his Dad's back because the pain was so intense.

A Face Radiant with God's Glory

I think Peter was the last one to pray. He said something like this:

> Lord, when I discovered I had cancer, the only thing
> I asked was that you might use this to honor and
> glorify your name. I thank you, Lord, that you have
> abundantly answered my prayer. If I make it, I will
> stand up and give you praise. But if I don't, I'll give
> you honor and glory till the very end.

As soon as the prayer meeting broke up, I sat down beside Peter and asked him how he was doing. The news was not good. A tumor had developed in his right lung, growing to the point it had shattered several of his ribs. That was why he was doubled over in pain.

Peter told me the doctors did not know for sure what kind of cancer this new tumor was. They told him it could be one of two kinds. "If it is one kind," he said, "I have two or three weeks to live. If it's the other kind, then I have one or two months."

He said it calmly, without fear or panic. In fact, he was smiling as he said it. As I looked at him, his face was radiant with the glory of God. Like Moses of old, my friend Peter had seen the Lord, and now nothing else mattered.

You Can't Trace God's Footsteps

He told me he preached the previous Sunday for the first time in seven weeks. They had to prop him up in his wheelchair, but he somehow found the strength to preach for an hour from Romans 11:33, "His paths (are) beyond tracing out." That text means you can't trace God's footsteps. *You don't know where he's come from, and you can't tell where he is going.* All you know is he is with you in the midst of your suffering.

The room was empty. All the other pastors were gone. Peter's last words to me were these: "All my life I've been speaking about

God's grace and trying to get people to listen. Now they listen when I speak because I've discovered that through it all, God's grace is sufficient." With that, his sons began to wheel him from the room. Though bent over with pain, he smiled and waved at me as he left.

The words of Paul came to my mind: "Though outwardly we are wasting away, yet inwardly we are being renewed day by day" (2 Corinthians 4:16).

And still the question remains. Why did my friend Peter die so young when he had so much to offer the world?

It is a mystery hidden in the mind and heart of God. *All human explanations must ultimately fail.* Is there an answer to the question "Why?" Yes, there is, but the answer is hidden from our view.

To all our questions, God replies, "I AM WHO I AM" (Exodus 3:14). *The answer is a Person, not an explanation.* Someone may reply, "But that's not enough. I want a real answer." To which I reply, "If God himself is not enough, then no answer would ever satisfy you."

The Ministry of Divine Comfort

But to leave the matter there would not be fair, for the Bible has a great deal to say about the ministry of divine comfort. It tells us many important truths we need to remember.

1. God himself draws near to those who hurt.

Psalm 34:18 says, "The Lord is close to the brokenhearted and saves those who are crushed in spirit." Here is a promise of God's special presence during our pain. Through the Holy Spirit, the Lord himself draws near to us in times of great suffering. We sense his presence in a way that goes beyond the natural. *We hear his voice though there is no sound in the room.* Many Christians can testify to this special sense of God's nearness felt during a time of great suffering.

2. God uses suffering to draw us to himself.

In this same Psalm, David declared, "I sought the Lord, and he answered me; he delivered me from all my fears" (v. 4). *Suffering*

turns us to the Lord as nothing else can. Perhaps you've heard it said
this way, "You never know if Jesus is all you need until Jesus is all
you have. And when Jesus is all you have, then and only then will
you discover Jesus really is all you need." Recently we received a
letter from a prisoner named Monica, who said,

> I finished reading *An Anchor for the Soul*, and I am
> about to begin reading it again … I truly believe I
> have been blessed by the situation I am currently in.
> Because of it I know I have gained eternal life with
> Jesus. If I had not been arrested, I doubt I would
> have ever come to know Jesus as I do now.

Prison is not "good" in the sense that we usually use the term,
but going to prison can be good if it causes us to turn to the Lord.
So it is with all the troubles, difficulties and afflictions of life. *We
pray more, and we pray more fervently during a time of crisis because
we know that if God doesn't help us, we're sunk.* Sometimes I think
God allows certain things to happen to his children in order to get
our attention focused completely on him.

3. We grow faster in hard times than we do in good times.

Romans 5:2–4 describes the process God uses to develop godly
character in our lives. In fact, Paul says "we also rejoice in our
sufferings" (v. 3). That may appear to be a misprint, but it isn't. Paul
isn't suggesting we should become masochists who rejoice in the hard
times as if we enjoyed the pain. That wouldn't be a Christian idea.
He doesn't say, "We rejoice *because of* our sufferings" but rather, "We
rejoice *in* our sufferings."

Even in the most difficult moments, God's people can rejoice
because he is at work doing something important in them. The
next few verses explain the process. Suffering produces perseverance,
perseverance produces character, character produces hope, and "hope
does not disappoint us because God has poured out his love into our

hearts by the Holy Spirit" (v. 5). *What starts with suffering ends with the love of God.* This is a wonderful progression, but you cannot get to the love of God without starting in the place of suffering.

More than one person has said to me, "I wouldn't trade my pain for the things God has shown me." If that doesn't make sense to you, it is only because you haven't been there yet.

4. Our sufferings qualify us to minister to others.

2 Corinthians 1:4 tells us that God "comforts us in all our troubles, so that we can comfort those in any trouble with the comfort we ourselves have received from God." The Greek word translated "comfort" in this verse is the same word Jesus used in Matthew 5:4. God uses our sufferings to comfort us so that when we are better, we can then minister to others in his name.

No one understands cancer like someone who has been through it. No one understands divorce like a person who's been through it. No one understands the pain of a miscarriage like a mother who has lost a child that way. No one knows the pain of losing a job like someone who has been told, "You're fired."

Many Christians are superbly qualified to minister to others, and they don't even know it. They are the ones who have been deeply hurt by the troubles of life, and through it all they have discovered God is faithful. Those folks have an important message to share. They can say with conviction, "God will take care of you. I know, because he took care of me."

They have earned their degree in the School of Suffering, and now they are qualified to minister to others who are newly enrolled.

The Majesty of God's Sovereignty

What do these things teach us about the character of God?

1. Because God is sovereign and we are not, most of our questions will never be answered in this life.

Some people can't live with that truth, so they devise human answers to explain suffering and death. Those answers rarely work, and sometimes they hurt more than they help. When I am called to the hospital, I never try to answer these hard questions. They are beyond me. Better to say less and be silent before the Lord than to try to explain the mysterious ways of God.

2. Because God is good, we know he has our best interests at heart.

That sentence gets to the heart of Romans 8:28. *The longer I live, the more I am convinced that the goodness of God is the central issue of life.* If you believe God is good, you can endure things that would break most people. You can live with unanswered questions so long as you believe in the goodness of God. But once you doubt his goodness, you must become either a secret atheist or an angry Christian. And really, there's not much difference in those two categories, if you think about it.

When our oldest son was in high school, he and a few friends survived a late-night wreck that totally destroyed our new van. The man at the local body shop estimated that when the van hit the tree, it was going at least 50 miles per hour. The force of the impact drove the engine eighteen inches off its block and into the passenger compartment. You could see tufts of hair in the windshield left from the force of the impact. In the providence of God, the van hit the tree in the center of the front bumper. "If it had hit the tree six inches to the left or right, you would have been going to the funeral home, not to the hospital," the man told us.

I cannot explain why things happened the way they did. At one point that night, there were four people in four different hospitals. But no one died, and we eventually replaced our van. Several months later, during a Thanksgiving service, my wife rose to give a testimony.

She said something like this: "Many of you know our oldest son and his friends barely survived a terrible wreck. Some people have told us God was good to spare Joshua and the others who were with him. It's true that God was good to us, but God would have been good even if Joshua had died in the wreck."

I confess I was unnerved when I heard those words. Like many people, I am accustomed to connecting God's goodness with my happiness. But it doesn't work that way. *God's character is not on trial in your sufferings.* You may think it is, but it isn't. Job tried to put God on trial, but the Lord ended up putting Job on trial.

God is good, and his mercy endures forever. That is true regardless of our experience.

3. Because God is wise, nothing is ever wasted in our experience.

Romans 8:29 tells us that God has predestined us to be conformed to the image of Jesus Christ. I often think of a sculptor sitting down before a hunk of marble. On the outside, the marble looks ugly and unformed. But the sculptor sees something beautiful inside that hunk. So with hammer and chisel, he begins to chip away. For many weeks he shapes, cuts, and polishes, until little by little an image emerges from the stone. On and on he works, never stopping until the sculpture is complete. What was once ugly is now a thing of beauty.

Even so, the Lord takes the hammer and chisel of human suffering to shape us into the image of Jesus Christ. In those moments when we feel that God has hammered us into the ground, we discover later that nothing was done in anger, nothing in haste, but everything was done according to his plan so that, in the end, we might be beautiful, like Jesus himself.

The most beautiful Christians I know are not the young, the rich, the educated, the successful, or the influential. Those men and women may be happy, but their lives are shallow because the sculptor has not yet picked up the hammer and the chisel. *No, the most beautiful Christians I know are those who have been through suffering and come through it with their faith in God intact.* They may not laugh as much as others, and their faces may be lined with care, but the beauty of Christ is in their eyes, and their voices testify to God's amazing grace.

If you feel the heavy weight of God hammering down on you, rest assured that nothing is being wasted. *Everything has a purpose.* In the end, God will be glorified, and you will be more beautiful than you ever dreamed possible.

4. Because God is love, he will not leave you alone in your pain.

This is the promise of the second Beatitude, "Blessed are those who mourn, for they will be comforted"(Matthew 5:4). *God will come to you.* You may not feel it or believe it, but it is true, for he has promised it. If it were necessary, I could produce a long line of witnesses who could testify to God's comfort in the midst of great suffering.

But it is not necessary to do that. *I know God will come to you because he came for you 2000 years ago.* God proved his love when he sent his Son Jesus into this sin-cursed world. He didn't have to do it. He chose to do it. He did what we would never do. He voluntarily sacrificed his only Son. He not only sent him to earth, he also watched Jesus die a terrible, bloody death.

After Calvary, God has nothing left to prove to anyone. How can you doubt his love after you look at the bleeding form of Jesus hanging on the cross?

> See from his head, his hands, his feet,
> Sorrow and love flow mingled down;
> Did e'er such love or sorrow meet,
> Or thorns compose so rich a crown?
> -Isaac Watts ("When I Survey the Wondrous Cross")

I realize this may not answer every question, but it does answer the most important question: Does God care for me in the midst of my suffering? The answer is yes, God cares for you, and if you doubt his love, fix your gaze on the cross and be comforted.

We understand these strange words a bit better when we see them refracted through the bloody haze of Good Friday. See him on the cross, "a man of sorrows, and acquainted with grief." He knows what you are going through. He will personally comfort you, and in the end, you will be blessed.

3

CAN WE STILL BELIEVE IN ROMANS 8:28?

Do all things really work together for good? Consider the following:

- A seemingly healthy 12-year-old girl develops severe migraine headaches. On Friday she is taken to the hospital; on Saturday she dies. Her father calls her "the sunshine of my life."
- A man feels the call of God to go into the ministry. He leaves his good job and moves to a distant city to enter seminary. His wife takes a job to help him make it through. He's in his last year now. In just a few months he'll take a church somewhere and begin serving the Lord. But one day his wife comes in and says, "I'm leaving you. I don't want to be a pastor's wife." She walks out and never comes back.
- A policeman stops a man known to be a drug dealer. It happens on a busy downtown street and a crowd gathers to watch the unfolding drama. There is a struggle and somehow the drug dealer grabs the officer's gun. Someone in the crowd

yells, "Shoot him, man." And he does, at point-blank range, in the face. The officer was in his early twenties.

Do all things work together for good? Do they? Can we still believe in Romans 8:28? Let me give you the verse the way I learned it, in the King James Version:

> And we know that all things work together for good to them that love God, to them who are the called according to his purpose.

Let us be honest and admit that we have at least two problems with these words by the apostle Paul.

1. They promise something we have trouble believing. Our text says, "And *we know* that all things work together for good" (KJV). Paul, how can you be so sure about that? Most of us are not as sure as Paul was. We hope all things work together for good; we believe they do. But do we really know that to be true?

2. They include things that we think ought to be left out. When Paul says, "*All things* work together for good," that seems too definite for us. All things? We might go so far as to say that "some things" work together for good. We understand that out of difficulty we learn great lessons of faith that cannot come any other way. Yes, some things clearly work together for good. But can we be sure it is really all things? Perhaps these words are true in the theoretical sense or perhaps as a statement of faith. But are they true to every part of life?

Romans 8:28 is one of the most beloved verses in the Bible. *You know that.* Many of you could give testimony to that fact. You were sick, and this verse was like medicine to your soul. You lost a loved one, and these words somehow carried you through. You were crushed and beaten by the winds of ill-fortune, and this verse gave you hope to go on.

Therefore, it shocks us to know that there are many who secretly doubt it. They hear this verse quoted, and instead of a balm to the soul, it seems like a mocking, cruel joke.

They say, "What do you mean by good?"

- Sickness is not good.
- Murder is not good.
- Divorce is not good.
- Suicide is not good.
- The death of a child is not good.

This verse is sometimes misused by well-meaning Christians who throw it in the face of those who are suffering as if it could answer every question of life. When it is misused that way, it produces an effect opposite to that intended by Paul.

But like it or not, it's in the Bible. And it won't go away. Which brings us back to the basic question: Can we still believe in Romans 8:28?

Four considerations will help us answer that question. These are four perspectives we need to keep in mind as we read this verse. *They are not original with me.* During my doctoral studies, I attended a seminar taught by Dr. Vernon Grounds, the longtime president of Denver Seminary. One afternoon he shared these insights with us, and I am simply passing them along to you.

We Must Start With God

Let's look at the first phrase in three different versions:

King James Version: "All things work together for good to them that love God."

New American Standard Bible: "God causes all things to work together for good."

New International Version: "In all things God works for the good of those who love him."

Did you catch the difference? In the King James version God is way down at the end of the phrase. *In the other two versions God is at the beginning.* It is partly a question of text and partly a question of grammar. There is nothing wrong with the traditional version, but the modern translations bring out a proper emphasis. *We will never understand this verse as long as we put God at the end and not at the beginning.* But some people look at life that way. They believe life is like a roll of the dice: sometimes you win and sometimes you lose. They believe that after a tragedy, God shows up to make everything come out right. But that is not the biblical view at all.

In reality, God is there at the beginning, he is there at the end, and he is there at every point in between. God is at work. Not luck, or chance, or blind fate. And that answers the great question, "Where is God when it hurts? Is he there at the beginning, or is he there only at the end?" The answer is that Romans 8:28 *begins* with God. He was there before it all happened, he is there when it happens, and he is still there after it is all over. That forever puts an end to the happy-ever-afterism that says, "No matter what happens, God will turn a tragedy into a blessing." That's fine for fairy tales, but not for real life.

What do you say when a little child dies? Or when a cop is killed by a drug dealer? Or when a man dies on the mission field? Or when a woman is cheated out of her inheritance? Or when a friend dies of cancer? Or when your marriage falls apart after 38 years? It is hard to see how these things are good.

When we look at these situations, we must at all costs resist the cheap explanation. It's too quick, too easy. When a tragedy happens, well-meaning people sometimes say, "That's not a tragedy. It only looks that way. Just have faith." If you believe tragedy is not really tragedy, you will probably lose your faith altogether.

Suppose I have an accident and wreck my car. And suppose when I take it into the body shop, the man says, "Friend, you haven't had an accident. Your car has just been rearranged." So I turn and look at the cracked grille, the crumpled fender, the twisted bumper, and the shattered windshield. Then I say, "Buddy, you're crazy. This car isn't rearranged. It's wrecked."

The Bible never asks us to pretend tragedy isn't tragedy or to pretend that our pain isn't real. *The point is, we must see the active involvement of God.* What happens to you and to me is not the mechanical turning of some impersonal wheel. It is not fate or karma or luck. God is actively at work in your life!

Is Paul saying, "Whatever happens is good"? No.
Is he saying suffering and evil and tragedy are good? No.
Is he saying everything will work out if we just have enough faith? No.
Is he saying we will understand why God allowed tragedy to come? No.

What, then, *is* he saying? He is erecting a sign over the unexplainable mysteries of life, a sign that reads, "Quiet. God at work." How? We're not always sure. To what end? Good, and not evil. That's what Romans 8:28 is saying.

Little children will often be afraid at night because they can't see in the darkness. They cry out until at last Daddy comes. He sits on the bed and takes them in his arms and holds them and says, "Don't be afraid. I'm right here with you." *The fear goes away when Daddy comes.* Even so, the darkness of life frightens us until we discover that our heavenly Father is there. The darkness is still dark, but he is with us, and that makes all the difference.

Can we still believe in Romans 8:28? Yes, but we need to start with God.

We Need a Long-Term Perspective

So many things in life seem unexplainable. Why does a tornado destroy one house and leave another untouched? Why does one brother excel while another struggles all his life? Why does a tumor come back when the doctor said he thought he got it all? The list of such questions is endless. Seen in isolation, they make no sense whatsoever. If there is a purpose behind such tragedy, we cannot see it. *Our danger is that we will judge the end by the beginning.* Or, to be more exact, we judge what we cannot see by what we can see. When tragedy strikes, if we can't see a purpose, we assume there isn't one.

But the very opposite is true. *We ought to judge the beginning by the end.* Here is where Romans 8:28 gives us some real help. Paul says, "And we know that all things *work together* for good." The phrase *work together* is really one word in Greek. We get our English word *synergy* from it. And what is synergy? It is what happens when you put two or more elements together to form something brand new that neither could form separately. It's what happens when my wife goes into the kitchen and makes a big pot of John Madden's Super Bowl Stew. She puts in the potatoes, the carrots, the celery, the rutabagas, the turnips, the spices, the meat, and a few other secret ingredients I know nothing about. What comes out is the best stew I've ever had. Left to myself I would never eat rutabagas or turnips. But in the Super Bowl Stew they combine with all those other ingredients to produce a gastronomic delight. That's synergy—the combination of many elements to produce a positive result.

That's what Paul means when he says God causes all things to "work together." *Many things that make no sense when seen in isolation are in fact working together to produce something good in my life.* There is a divine synergy even in the darkest moments, a synergy that produces something positive. And the "good" that is ultimately produced could not happen any other way.

A few years ago Toyota opened a huge automobile plant outside of Tupelo, Mississippi. I got a bird's-eye view when our plane flew right over the plant. What you see are two vast buildings that cover many acres. Day and night the trucks bring in the raw materials and various component parts of an automobile: the engine, the wheels, the chassis, the frame, the outer body, the windshield, the instrument panel, the seats, the carpeting, and so on. All of that goes into the plant and becomes part of the assembly line. At the end of the line a new Toyota Corolla rolls out.

Now suppose you decided to watch the process from the road. You would see the trucks arriving with the component parts, and you would see the new cars rolling out the door. What happens in between? *From the outside you can't tell.* You hear the noise from within, but you cannot see the process. But you know this much: That new car did not happen by chance. Inside the building intelligent minds and capable hands take the raw material and the component parts and from them fashion a car. What seemed to have no purpose turns out to be indispensable.

Our experience is like that. God begins with the raw materials of life, including some parts that seem to serve no good purpose. Those materials are acted upon by pressure and heat and then are bent and shaped and joined together. *Over time something beautiful is created.* Not by accident, but by divine design. And nothing is wasted in the process.

That is how we must look at life. We must not judge the end by the beginning, but rather the beginning by the end.

Can we still believe in Romans 8:28? Yes, we can. But we need a long-term perspective.

We Must Define the Word "Good"

This is the crux of the matter. Paul says "all things work together for good." But what is the "good" he is talking about? For most of us, "good" equals things like health, happiness, solid relationships, long life, money, food on the table, meaningful work, and a nice place to live. In general, we think the "good" life means a better set of circumstances.

Once again, that's not necessarily the biblical viewpoint. In this case we don't have to wonder what Paul means. He defines it for us in the very next verse: "For those God foreknew he also predestined to be conformed to the likeness of his Son" (Romans 8:29). That makes it very clear. God has predestined you and me to a certain end. That certain end is the "good" of Romans 8:28. It is that we might be conformed to the likeness of Jesus Christ.

Let me put it plainly. *God is at work in your life making you like Jesus Christ.* He has predestined you to that end. Therefore, anything that makes you more like Jesus Christ is good. Anything that pulls you away from Jesus Christ is bad. When Paul says all things work together for good, he is not saying that the tragedies and heartaches of life will always produce a better set of circumstances. Sometimes they do, sometimes they don't. But God is not committed to making you happy and successful. He *is* committed to making you like his Son, the Lord Jesus Christ. And whatever it takes to make you more like Jesus is good.

God has arranged things so that we learn more in the darkness than we do in the light. We gain more from sickness than we do from health. We pray more when we are scared than when we are confident. And everything that happens to you—the tragedies, the unexplained circumstances, even the stupid choices you make—all of it is grist for the mill of God's loving purpose. He will not give up even when we do.

Robert Browning Hamilton said it this way:

> I walked a mile with Pleasure,
> She chattered all the way.
> But I was none the wiser,
> For all she had to say.
>
> Then I walked a mile with Sorrow,
> And ne'er a word said she.
> But, oh, the lessons I did learn
> When Sorrow walked with me.

God is at work in your life. Right now, you are rough and uncut, and God is patiently chipping away at you. But remember this: He will never intentionally hurt you. *In the end, you will look like the Lord Jesus Christ.*

This, I think, is our greatest problem with Romans 8:28. *Our good and God's good are not the same.* We want happiness and fulfillment and peace and long life. Meanwhile, God is at work in us and through us and by everything that happens to us to transform us into the image of his Son.

Does that include the worst that happens to us? Yes.
Does that include the things that hurt us deeply? Yes.
Does that include the times when we are heartbroken? Yes.
Does that include the times when we sin? Yes.
Does that include the times when we doubt God? Yes.
Does that include the times when we curse him to his face? Yes.

He is always at work. He is never deterred by us. *Nothing happens to us outside his control.* There are no mistakes and no surprises.

God can do that even when we can't.
God does it even when we don't believe it.

That is what Paul means when he says, "We know." We know it because we know God, and he has said it. His word is trustworthy, and that guarantees it. Indeed, his character rests upon it.

We know it not by looking at the events of life, but by knowing God. We know it not by studying the pattern of the cloth, but by knowing the designer of the fabric. We know it not by listening to the notes of the symphony, but by knowing the composer of the music.

There are many things we don't know. We don't know why babies die or why cars wreck or why planes crash or why families break up or why good people get sick and suddenly die. But this we do know: God is at work, and he has not forgotten us.

Can we still believe in Romans 8:28? Yes, but we must properly define what "good" means.

We Must Understand the Limitation of This Verse

Notice the last phrase of Romans 8:28. It is a promise to "those who love God, who have been called according to his purpose." That is an all-important limitation. *This verse is true of Christians and only of Christians.* It is not a blanket promise to the whole human race. Why? Because God's purpose is to make his children one day like his Son.

Therefore, we may say Romans 8:28 is an evangelistic verse. And we can ask two simple questions:

1. Have you ever responded to God's call?
2. Are you part of God's saving purpose?

You either answer yes or no to those questions. There is no middle ground. Until you can answer yes, this verse does not apply to you.

Here's a prisoner letter we received not long after *An Anchor for the Soul* was published.

Dear Ray Pritchard,

I have some "Good News" and some "Not-so-Good-News" that I would like to share with you. First, the "not so Good News." This is not my first time, second time, or my fifth time, but somewhere around my tenth time that I have been locked up at the county jail. I have been to prison three times. I was released with two years of parole. A year went by, and I again was arrested and charged with burglary. So here I am, charged with burglary, on parole for burglary, and my entire life is burglary (5 to be exact). I am sure you would say to me that I need to change "careers." I am looking at 6 to 30 years of prison time.

Now the "Good News." My cellmate, Charles, offered a book for me to read. The title of the book is *An Anchor for the Soul* by (none other than) Ray Pritchard. I have read it from front to back. I have heard the "knock on the door," I have "went to the door," and "I have finally opened it."

I HAVE LET CHRIST INTO MY HEART.

I wake to a morning prayer and end my day with prayer. During my day I practice what you have preached. I know I will be distracted by the devil, and conflicts will arise most likely when everything is going smooth.

To end my letter to you, I cannot say "Thank You" enough for sharing the knowledge and encouragement to seek God. I truly believe your book will have great impact on the rest of my life as long as I continue to "open the door" and let Christ in every day. I believe I will then never, ever have to be locked up physically or spiritually again.

He signed the letter "A grateful recovering alcohol/drug addict." Then he added this P.S.: "I have thanked you, I have thanked Jesus. I believe it is time to thank my cellmate, Charles."

Going to prison is not "good" in the usual sense of the word. But it is better to be in prison and to find Jesus than to be free on the outside and trapped by sin on the inside. This letter shows how Romans 8:28 works even in the hard times of life.

Two Important Qualifications

And so we come back to the basic question: Can we still believe in Romans 8:28? It sounds good.

We want to believe it.

We can believe in Romans 8:28 as long as we keep two things in mind.

1. We must not try to explain the unexplainable.

Sometimes in our zeal to protect God, we try to explain why bad things happen to good people. *That's almost always a bad idea.* We are like little children looking into the face of an infinitely wise Father. It is not possible that we should understand all he does. It is enough that we love him and know he is there.

Let us be honest and confess it is right at this point so much damage has been done. In the end, it is not this verse that has lost its credibility, but rather our feeble attempts to justify the mysterious ways of God. *Better to say nothing than to speak of things we know nothing about.*

2. We must understand that God's values and our values are not the same.

This is really like saying, "We must understand that we will often not understand at all." Let's be clear on this point. We are not called to praise God for evil, sin, and death. *But we can praise God for the good he can work in the darkest days of life.* Romans 8:28 is not teaching us to call evil good or simply to smile through the tears and pretend everything is OK. But it *is* teaching us that no matter what happens to us, no matter how terrible, no matter how unfair, our God is there. He has not left us. His purposes are being worked out as much in the darkness as they are in the light.

"Where Was God When My Son Died?"

The story is told of a father whose son was killed in a terrible accident. He came to his pastor and in great anger said, "Where was God when my son died?" The pastor thought for a moment and replied, "The same place he was when his Son died." *That's the final piece of the puzzle.* He knows what we are going through for he has been there. He watched his own Son die.

Therefore, we can say with the apostle Paul, "We know." Not because we see the answer, but because we know him, and he knows what it is like to lose a Son. He knows, and we know him.

Can we still believe in Romans 8:28? If you don't believe this verse, what is your alternative? If you don't believe in Romans 8:28, what do you believe in? Fate? Chance? The impersonal forces of nature?

Yes, we can—and must—believe in Romans 8:28. It is teaching us one great truth: *All things ultimately contribute to the ultimate good of those who love God.*

That does not answer every question. But it does answer the big question: Does God know what he is doing? Yes, he does, and we know him, and that is enough.

4

THE MYSTERY OF UNANSWERED PRAYER

"You won't believe the things that have happened to me."

The man stood over my desk as he spoke those words. Then he proceeded to tell a tale of woe the likes of which I had not heard in many years. As I listened, it seemed to boil down to three basic parts. First, he had lost his promising career through a complicated series of cunning plots against him. Then his wife left him for greener pastures and more security. And now he was facing a mountain of legal bills. He seemed to be backed into a corner. His question was simple: Why would God let something like this happen to me?

The phone rang about nine o'clock one night. The voice at the other end said, "Pastor Pritchard, could I talk to you for a few minutes?" As I listened, I heard a story about a marriage gone bad. She had married him a few years earlier, and things had not gone well. He abused her, and later he abused the kids. Eventually she filed for divorce, and now he wants nothing to do with her or the children. In her heart of hearts, her greatest desire is for God to give her someone to be a loving husband and godly father. She has prayed and prayed about it, but there seems to be no answer. "Pastor Pritchard, why doesn't God answer my prayers? Is he punishing me because I got a divorce?"

Another phone call came.

A woman in our congregation had a stroke. When I finally got to the hospital, she couldn't talk, but she could squeeze my hand. "This is Pastor Ray. Do you recognize me?" She did. I prayed for her, and then I said, "Don't worry. You're going to be all right. We're going to pray you through this." The whole church prayed for her, but things weren't all right. That night she had another stroke, this time a massive hemorrhage that left her comatose. Five days later she died. In the end, our prayers seemed to make no difference.

Where Is God When We Need Him?

Of all the things that weigh us down, perhaps no burden is greater than the silence of God.

- A godly mother prays for her wayward son. He was raised in the church, he went to Sunday school, he knows the Bible, but when he left home, he left it all behind. For many years his mother has prayed for him, but to this day he remains a prodigal son.

- A wife prays for her husband, who left her after 23 years of marriage for a younger woman. He seems utterly unreachable, and the marriage heads swiftly for divorce.

- A husband prays for his wife, who has terminal cancer. She has six, maybe seven months to live. None of the treatments stop the rampaging tumors. The elders anoint her with oil and pray over her in the name of the Lord. She dies five months later.

- A young man prays fervently for deliverance from an overpowering temptation, but the struggle never seems to end. The more he prays, the worse the temptation becomes.

And so we cry out with the psalmist, "Why, O Lord, do you stand far off? Why do you hide yourself in times of trouble?" (Psalm 10:1).

The Problem No One Talks About

As we think about this question, we will be helped if we acknowledge reality. *A great many believers struggle with the issue of unanswered prayer.* If there is a God, if he really does answer prayer, why doesn't he answer my prayers?

For those who are in pain, a theoretical answer will not suffice. Nor will it be enough to simply say, "God always answers prayer. Sometimes he says yes, sometimes he says no, and sometimes he says wait awhile." We say this a lot. I've said it myself. But it sounds facile and superficial when someone cries out to God from the pit of despair, and the heavens are as brass, and the answer never comes.

Some people bear hidden scars from the pain of prayers that were not answered. They remember times when they prayed, really prayed, said all the right words with all the right motives, even asked their friends to join them in prayer, deeply believing that only God could help them out; and after they prayed, they waited and waited and waited, but God never seemed to answer.

We don't talk about this problem very much. I suppose that's because we're afraid if we admit our prayers aren't always answered, it will cause some people to lose their faith in God. As a matter of fact, that's exactly what has happened. *Many good, devout people secretly doubt God answers prayer.* They doubt it, for when it really counted, God did not come through for them. So in their hearts, deep in the inner recesses of the soul, hidden behind a smiling face, rests a profound disenchantment with the Almighty.

Calvin and Hobbes

You wouldn't think such a serious subject would make it to the comics, but I happened to find it in a comic strip called *Calvin and Hobbes*. It's late November, and a little boy is waiting with his sled for the first big snowfall. He waits and waits, but all he finds is brown grass and no snow.

So he says, "If I was in charge, we'd never see grass between October and May." Then, looking to the heavens, he says, "On 'three,' ready? One … Two … Three. SNOW!" Nothing happens, and the little boy is downcast. Then he shouts to the heavens, "I said snow! C'mon! Snow!" Then, shaking his fists, he cries, "SNOW!" Now thoroughly disgusted with God's failure, he says, "OK then, don't snow! See what I care! I like this weather! Let's have it forever!" But his defiance does not last. In the next frame we see the little boy on his knees offering this prayer: "Please snow! Please?? Just a foot! OK, eight inches! That's all! C'mon! Six inches, even! How about just six??" Then he looks to heaven and shouts, "I'm WAAIITING …"

In the next frame we see him running in a circle, head down, fists clenched, making a little-boy sound which the artist spells out as "RRRRGGHHH." That's not an English word, but every parent has heard it many times. Finally, the little boy is exhausted, his energy spent, his prayer unanswered, with snow nowhere in sight. In the final frame, he looks up at God and cries out in utter desperation, "Do you want me to become an atheist?"

Many Christians feel just like that little boy, only they have prayed for things much more important than a few inches of snow, but the end result has been the same. In their frustration and despair, they have cried out to God, "Do you want me to become an atheist?" Some of them have. Most haven't, but they keep the pain inside, still believing as best they can in a God who sometimes answers prayer and sometimes doesn't.

When Dad Died

At this point I would like to add my own testimony to the list. Many years ago, my father suddenly and inexplicably became very ill. I was just married and was starting seminary when I got the late-night call from my mom. My father was so sick they had taken him to a hospital in Birmingham. Marlene and I made the trip from Dallas, and the whole thing was like a dream to me. My dad was a doctor. Doctors don't get sick; they heal the sick. How could *my* dad be in the hospital? But he was, and the outlook was not good. Something about a strange bacterial infection the doctors could not stop.

And so began a two-week ordeal I will never forget. We went to Birmingham and then back to Dallas. A few days later the call came, and we went back again. This time Dad was worse. I prayed, but it was hard, and I was scared.

The turning point came on the second trip when I went in to see my father in intensive care. By this time, he was in and out of a coma, and I don't think he knew who I was. When I went back out in the hallway, I saw a friend from my childhood days. He had come down to see how I was doing. Something about seeing an old friend triggered my emotions, and I collapsed against the wall and began to weep. In that terrible moment that I realized my father was dying, and I could do nothing about it.

A few days later, my father died despite our prayers and the doctors' best efforts. Forty-five years have passed, and I know many things now I didn't know then. I understand life a little better. But after all these years, I still don't know why God didn't answer our prayers. The mystery is as great to me today as it was in the hospital corridor in Birmingham, Alabama. I didn't know then, and I don't know now.

My Grace Is Sufficient

But I have been helped by one great discovery: *I'm not the first person to have my prayers go unanswered.* In fact, the Bible is filled with stories of men and women who prayed to God in the moment of crisis, and God—for reasons sometimes explained and more often not explained—did not answer their prayers. We don't hear much about that because our focus is naturally on the great answers that came just in the nick of time. Most of us would rather hear about the parting of the Red Sea than about Trophimus being left sick at Miletus. *Miracles that did happen are more encouraging than stories of miracles that almost happened.*

As I flip through the pages of the Bible, I find no story of unanswered prayer that encourages me more than the account of Paul's unanswered prayer in 2 Corinthians 12. In that passage Paul reveals that 14 years earlier, he had been caught up into heaven and had seen things no mortal man had ever seen before. It was a profound experience that he never forgot. But when that great experience was over, something else happened to Paul that would change his whole perspective on life. Let him tell the story in his own words:

> "To keep me from becoming conceited because of these surpassingly great revelations, there was given me a thorn in my flesh, a messenger of Satan, to torment me" (2 Corinthians 12:7).

Bible students are divided about what this verse really means. Some suggest the "thorn in the flesh" was the fierce opposition Paul received from his Jewish opponents. Others suggest it was demonic oppression. Still others think the thorn was a physical ailment that crippled Paul in some way and limited his effectiveness.

In one sense it doesn't matter. The crucial point is that Paul prayed for God to remove the "thorn in his flesh" so that he could get on with his ministry. In fact he prayed not once, but three times. Each time God said no: "Three times I pleaded with the Lord to take it away from me" (v. 8).

Can you imagine that? The apostle Paul, probably the greatest Christian who ever lived, the man who introduced Christianity to Europe, the man who wrote so much of the New Testament—that man, when he prayed about this need in his life, found that God did not, *would* not, answer his prayers.

It's hard to believe because we know Paul was a man of prayer. He writes about prayer in all his letters. Suppose Paul were to come to your church next Sunday and after the service said, "Now, I'll be glad to pray for any of you." What would you do? I know what I'd do. I'd get in line and ask Paul to pray for me.

But here's a clear-cut case, given in his own words, of a time in his life when he desperately begged God over and over again to answer a very specific prayer, and God said no.

As I ponder this story, I gather great encouragement from it. It teaches me several important principles:

1. **Unanswered prayer happens to the very best Christians.**
2. **When it happens, it is humanly unexplainable.**
3. **When it happens, God has a higher purpose in mind.**

In Paul's case he kept on praying until God finally gave him an explanation. "But he said to me, 'My grace is sufficient for you, for my power is made perfect in weakness'" (v. 9).

Sometimes our prayers are not answered because God can do more through us by not answering our prayers than he can by answering them.

Sometimes God's no is better than his yes.

Think of it this way. What would happen if God answered all your prayers all the time in the exact way you prayed? Forget for a moment that some of your prayers are foolish and shortsighted. Just suppose God answered them all. Would that produce spiritual maturity in your life? I think not. If God always answered your prayers, eventually your trust would be in the answers and not in the Lord alone.

But when God says no, we are forced to decide whether we will still trust in God alone—without the benefit of an answered prayer to lean upon.

Don't get me wrong. Answered prayer is amazing, and if *none* of our prayers were answered we would probably stop praying altogether. But if all our prayers were answered, we would end up taking God for granted. *Unanswered prayer forces us to trust in God alone.* When we do, he alone gets the glory, for it is at that point his strength is made perfect in our weakness.

We Grow Best in the Darkness

When he was an old man looking back on his life, British journalist Malcolm Muggeridge summarized it this way in an interview with William F. Buckley:

> As an old man, Bill, looking back on one's life, it's one of the things that strike you most forcibly— that the only thing that's taught one anything is suffering. Not success, not happiness, not anything like that. The only thing that really teaches one what life's about—the joy of understanding, the joy of coming in contact with what life really signifies—is suffering, affliction (William F. Buckley, "Malcolm Muggeridge and the Longing for Faith," *Washington Post*, Nov. 24, 1990).

This is exactly what Paul is saying, and it is the testimony of Christians across the centuries. *We grow best in the darkness of pain, sadness and despair.* We learn many things in the sunlight, but we grow best in the darkness.

Sometimes it is better for us if our prayers are not answered immediately. Sometimes it is better if they are not answered at all. The great question is not, "How can I get my prayers answered?" The great question is, "What will it take to draw me closer to God?"

Consider these words by Edgar Guest:

> I asked God for strength, that I might achieve;
> I was made weak, that I might learn humbly to obey.
> I asked for health, that I might do greater things;
> I was given infirmity, that I might do better things.
> I asked for riches, that I might be happy;

I was given poverty, that I might be wise.
I asked for power, that I might have the praise of men;
I was given weakness, that I might feel the need of God.
I asked for all things, that I might enjoy life;
I was given life, that I might enjoy all things.
I got nothing I asked for, but everything I had hoped for.
Almost despite myself, my unspoken prayers were answered.
I am, among men, most richly blessed.

It is a great advance in spiritual understanding to be able to say,
"I got nothing I asked for, but everything I had hoped for."

Though He Slay Me

Sometimes our prayers will go unanswered. Unless you admit that
fact and deal with it as a Christian, you will probably give up prayer
altogether. To make matters worse, sometimes our prayers offered
from righteous motives and pure hearts will seem to accomplish
nothing. It is as if the heavens have turned to brass.

But that is not true. *God hears every prayer, even the ones he chooses
not to answer.* No prayer is entirely wasted, for even unanswered
prayer may be used by God to draw us closer to him. In that case
we may say it was better for our prayers to go unanswered that we
might draw near to God.

The final solution lies somewhere along these lines: *When we pray,
we tend to focus exclusively on the answers; God wants us to focus on
him.* Whatever will help us do that is what we really need. Sometimes
our prayers will be answered in amazing and miraculous ways; other
times our prayers will not be answered at all.

Do you remember the experience of Job? He lost his home, his
fortune, his children, his health, and his reputation. All that he
counted dear was taken away from him. When he finally hit bottom,
filled with anger and wishing he were dead, he uttered these words
of faith: "Though he slay me, yet will I trust in him" (Job 13:15

KJV). It's as if he is saying to God, "You can take my life, but you can't make me stop trusting in you." Yes, there is a note of belligerent defiance in those words, and yes, Job wasn't too happy about what God had done to him. And yes, he wanted his day in court. But underneath the anger and searing pain was a bedrock faith in God: "I don't understand this at all, but I'm hanging on to you, Lord, and I'm not going to let go."

That's where God wants to bring us. Sometimes unanswered prayer is the only way to get us there.

When Your Prayers Are Not Answered

Having said all of that, we still need to know how to respond when we pray and God does not answer us. What do we do? I have three suggestions to make.

1. Keep on praying as long as you can.

Sometimes God's answers are delayed for reasons beyond our knowledge. Who can really say why a prayer which has been uttered 9,999 times should finally be answered on the 10,000th time? But sometimes it happens.

From time to time we hear stories of how people have prayed for a loved one for 20 or 30 years before the answer finally came. We all know of stories of how some people have made miraculous recoveries after the doctors had given up all hope. Should not we gain hope from such seeming miracles?

A woman stood up in a Sunday school class I was teaching and told about a friend (well-known to several others in our class) who had prayed for her husband's salvation for 59 years. After all those years, he finally trusted Christ and died a few months later. Don't you think his wife must have gotten discouraged somewhere along the way? What if she had stopped praying after 37 years?

So pray, pray, and keep on praying. As you pray, don't be ashamed to beg God for a miracle. I often tell people in a hard place, "If you need a miracle, ask for one. There's no extra charge for large requests."

Who knows? You may be surprised to find that in the end, after you have given up all hope, God has moved from heaven to answer your prayers in ways you never dreamed possible.

2. Give God the right to say no.

In the ultimate sense, God already has that right, whether you acknowledge it or not. But if you never acknowledge that God has the right to say no to you, you will be filled with anger, frustration, and despair. To fight against God's right to say no to you is really the same thing as fighting against God. That's a battle you'll never win.

How much better to say, "Lord, I am praying this prayer from the bottom of my heart, but even as I pray I confess that you have the right to say no if that's what you think is best." You'll sleep well at night when you learn to pray like that.

And in this we have the example of the Lord Jesus who, when he prayed in the Garden of Gethsemane with the sweat pouring off him like great drops of blood, said, "O my Father, if it be possible, let this cup pass from me: nevertheless not as I will, but as thou wilt" (Matthew 26:39 KJV). If Jesus needed to pray that way, how much more do we?

Let God be God in your life. Give him the right to say no.

3. Keep on doing what you know to be right.

In the darkness of unanswered prayer, you may be tempted to give up on God. You may feel like throwing in the towel and checking out of the Christian life. But what good will that do? If you turn away from God, where will you go?

Keep on praying, keep on believing, keep on reading the Bible, keep on obeying, keep on following the Lord. If you stay on course in the darkness, eventually the light will shine again, and you will be glad you did not turn away in the moment of disappointment.

He Maketh No Mistake

In the early years of the 20th century, a man named A. M. Overton pastored a small church in Mississippi. When his wife died during childbirth, he asked a pastor friend to speak at her funeral. While he was speaking, the pastor noticed Mr. Overton sitting in the pew writing something. Thinking that was a strange thing to do, he asked him about it after the service. He said he had been writing down a poem during the funeral service. "He Maketh No Mistake" has become very popular and has spread around the world.

Born out of deepest personal sorrow, it touches us with a profound statement of trust in God amid the trials of life.

> My Father's way may twist and turn,
> My heart may throb and ache
> But in my soul I'm glad I know,
> He maketh no mistake.
>
> My cherished plans may go astray,
> My hopes may fade away,
> But still I'll trust my Lord to lead
> For He doth know the way.
>
> Tho' night be dark and it may seem
> That day will never break,
> I'll pin my faith, my all in him,
> He maketh no mistake.
>
> There's so much now I cannot see,
> My eyesight's far too dim;
> But come what may, I'll simply trust
> And leave it all to him.

For by and by the mist will lift
And plain it all he'll make,
Through all the way, tho' dark to me,
He made not one mistake.

In the end that will be the testimony of every child of God. When we finally get to heaven, we'll look back over the pathway of life and see that through all the twists and turns and seeming detours that "he made not one mistake."

We see dimly now as we march on through the shadows of life. *But the day will come when the sunlight of God's love surrounds us as we stand in the presence of Jesus who loved us and gave himself for us.* Until then, we move on through the twilight, knowing that some of our prayers will not be answered no matter how hard we pray. But this fact sustains us on our long journey home: He did not say, "My answers are sufficient," but rather "My grace is sufficient for you."

5

FEAR NOT!

What are you afraid of?

Caty Medrano published an article called "Top 10 Strong Human Fears." These are the top fears shared by people everywhere. The list in many ways is self-explanatory.

10. Losing your freedom
9. The unknown
8. Pain
7. Disappointment
6. Misery
5. Loneliness
4. Ridicule
3. Rejection
2. Death
1. Failure

Many of these fears are tied together, such as death and the unknown, rejection and ridicule, pain and misery, and failure and loneliness. *We can also observe that these are mostly existential fears that describe an inner condition of the heart.* That is, these are not fears of specific things. In the latter category, I ran across a Gallup

Poll answering the question, "What scares Americans most?" In order the answers are:

1. Snakes
2. Public speaking
3. Heights
4. Being closed in a small space
5. Spiders
6. Needles and getting shots
7. Mice
8. Flying on an airplane
9. Dogs
10. Thunder and lightning
11. Going to the doctor
12. The dark

This is obviously a much more concrete list. I can identify with the part about snakes, heights, needles, and spiders. I fly so much that airplanes don't bother me, and I speak so much that while I do get nervous sometimes, I don't "fear" public speaking. I have no clue how dogs could possibly make that list. And while I may not fear the dark, I sometimes find little noises waking me up with a start in the middle of the night.

We all have our fears, don't we?

Your list won't be same as mine, but we can all identify with some things on the second list and most of the first list. *If we aren't worried about mice, we certainly fear rejection by those we love.* We all think about our own death from time to time. When will it happen and under what circumstances? If we are wise, we also wonder, what then?

I'm not surprised fear of failure comes at the top for many people. *No one wants to come to the end of life and feel like you've wasted your short sojourn on planet earth.* It's a terrible thing to conclude your life was a bust because it didn't turn out the way you hoped it would.

Somewhere in all our thinking God must figure into the equation. There must be a reason the Bible tells us (in various ways and in various places) to "fear not" hundreds of times. *Fear is such a basic human emotion that many of us constantly live in the grip of worry and anxiety.* God told us to "fear not" because he knew we would all wrestle with fear sooner or later.

What do you do when your fears seem to be winning the day? What if you pray and God still hasn't come through for you? If you are like most people, you begin to lose hope. And you wonder why you bothered to pray in the first place. Deep in the soil of your heart, little seeds of doubt take root, growing up into a harvest of frustration and anger.

It happens to most of us eventually. Even some of the best men and women of the Bible struggled with their inner doubts when their dreams didn't come true.

Waiting for a Baby

Abraham's story illustrates that truth. In order to get the context, we must go back 40 centuries, back to a time long ago and far away, to a place called Ur of the Chaldees, a large city on the banks of the Euphrates River. That river still exists. It flows through Iraq and empties into the Persian Gulf not far from Kuwait.

Historians tell us Ur was one of the most important cities of the ancient world. In Abraham's day perhaps 250,000 people lived there. There was an ancient university in Ur and a large library. Ur was known as a center for mathematics, astronomy, and international commerce. It was like Chicago or New York or London or Singapore.

What else do we know about Abraham (he is first called Abram, and later Abraham) as the story begins? He's about 75 years old when we meet him, which in those days would be considered middle-aged. He's a prosperous businessman who is no doubt well-known to many people. He and his wife Sarah (first called Sarai) have no children.

Against that backdrop God speaks to Abraham for the first time in Genesis 12:1-3:

> The Lord had said to Abram, "Leave your country, your people and your father's household and go to the land I will show you. I will make you into a great nation and I will bless you; I will make your name great and you will be a blessing. I will bless those who bless you, and whoever curses you I will curse; and all peoples on earth will be blessed through you."

Later God promised to give him descendants "like the dust of the earth" (Genesis 13:16). Ten years quickly pass without any sign of children. Abraham is almost 85 and not getting any younger. Sarah is far past childbearing age. Even though he has just won a great victory (see Genesis 14), nothing can satisfy his deep desire for a son.

Only those who have gone through this experience can fully empathize with Abraham and Sarah. *There is no sadness like the sadness of wanting children of your own but being unable to have them.* Even in this day of modern medicine and advanced technology, many couples wait for years, and some couples wait forever.

I think Abraham's greatest fear stemmed from the fact God did not seem in a hurry to give them a child. How much longer would he wait? Why had he delayed? Had God changed his mind? Was there some problem Abraham didn't know about? Had they sinned? Were they doing something displeasing to God? Why was Sarah's womb still closed? If God had promised, why was it taking so long to be fulfilled? Should they go to plan B? All those questions were running through Abraham's mind. *God knew exactly what his servant was thinking.* He saw the doubt and understood the fear. Now he moves to reassure Abraham all will be well. The time has not yet come for the child to be born, but it isn't far off either.

"I Am Your Shield"

After this, the word of the Lord came to Abram in a vision: 'Do not be afraid, Abram, I am your shield, your very great reward' (Genesis 15:1).

There are at least four reasons Abraham could have doubted God's promise of a son:

1. He was too old.
2. Too many years had passed since the promise had been given.
3. Nothing like this had ever happened before.
4. Sarah also doubted God's promise.

When you think about it, there was no reason to believe—no reason except God had promised to do it. The question now is simple: Will God's promise be enough for Abraham?

In answer to that question, God declares, "I am your shield." We should not think of a small shield that covers only the chest area, but of a shield that stretches from head to toe and protects every part of the soldier's body. Such a shield offers complete protection from every attack of the enemy.

To call God our shield means two specific things:

1. He protects us in times of doubt.
2. He rescues us in times of danger.

Note that God does not say, "I will give you a shield," but "I am your shield." The God of heaven says he will be our shield, which means we have a shield that is omnipotent, universal, eternal. That shield cannot be defeated because it is as strong as God himself.

We could not be in a better position. Who can defeat us when God himself is our shield?

The great message is certainly clear. If God is your shield, fear not!

Immortal Until

It has been said that "a Christian is immortal until his work on earth is done." *That statement means that nothing can harm you without God's permission.* Not cancer, not AIDS, not bankruptcy, not theft, not physical disability, not the loss of your job, not a terrible accident, not the death of a child, not any of a thousand other sorrows that afflict the children of God. Christians aren't immune to sadness. What happens to others also happens to us. The difference is this: *We know God protects us from harm so that nothing can touch us that doesn't first pass through his hands of love.* That doesn't mean that we don't weep or we don't suffer. Far from it. But it is the basis for the statement that we do not grieve like those who have no hope (1 Thessalonians 4:13). Our sorrow is different precisely because we hope in God.

A missionary told me how she had nearly been put in jail when a hostile lawyer began harassing her and the local Christian hospital. He objected to the fact the hospital openly did evangelism along with its compassionate medical care. Seeking a pretext for legal action, the lawyer accused the hospital of illegally selling intravenous fluid to its patients. It wasn't true, but that didn't matter. For nearly ten years the case bumped up and down the court system of that country. At one point it appeared likely the missionary might either be thrown in jail or forced to leave the country. "I'm going to shut down this hospital," the lawyer chortled, "And you're going to jail, or I'll have you deported." To which the missionary replied, "You can do nothing to me except what my God permits you to do."

That's a perfectly biblical answer. *Our God is a shield around his people.* Nothing can touch us except that which God permits.

Why God Delays His Answers

That brings us back to the central issue of this chapter. Why did God wait so long to give Abraham a son? Abraham was 75 when

God first spoke to him and 100 when Isaac was finally born. He was almost 85 when God came to him and said, "Fear not." After all those years God still wasn't ready to answer Abraham's prayers. Abraham was old, but he would be older yet before Isaac was finally born.

Few things are more vexing to the people of God than the question of unanswered prayer. We know God loves us and has a good plan for our lives. Why then does God take so long to answer our deepest, most heartfelt prayers? From Abraham's experience we may suggest three answers:

1. To develop perseverance in us.

To put it very simply, it would be too easy if God answered all our prayers the first time we prayed them. Not only would we take God for granted, but we would also develop a shallow faith.

I have a good friend who is stuck in a difficult job situation. She works with a colleague who has a reputation for being an easygoing, nice guy. "But he's not like that behind the scenes," she says. Every time she has a good idea, he either steals it or complains to the boss. Since his job is more important than hers, he always wins. He also uses threats and intimidation to get his way. He thinks only of himself and how he can get ahead, and he doesn't mind being ruthless if that's what it takes to get what he wants.

Sound familiar? Every office probably has a person who answers to that description. When I asked my friend if she was planning on leaving her job, she gave a very wise answer: "I know God put me here and gave me the talent to do my job. If he wants to move me, that's fine, but I'm not going to try to do it myself. I'm sure God can use me in this position, and I want to learn everything he is trying to teach me."

Here is a woman whose faith is growing stronger through a difficult situation. Every day she is being given new opportunities to trust God and to respond graciously to an unkind coworker. *Meanwhile, she prays for God to work in her and through her and, if necessary, to change her situation.* I believe God will eventually answer her prayers by either moving her on to a new job or by removing the other person. But that may not happen for months or years, and until then, my friend is developing many godly qualities as she patiently waits on the Lord.

2. To ensure that God alone gets the glory.

When Paul wrote about Abraham's story, he mentioned this point prominently. Romans 4:19-21 says,

> Without weakening in his faith, he faced the fact that his body was as good as dead—since he was about a hundred years old—and that Sarah's womb was also dead. Yet he did not waver through unbelief regarding the promise of God, but was strengthened in his faith and gave glory to God, being fully persuaded that God had power to do what he had promised.

Not only did Abraham have to wait 25 years for an answer to his prayers, but he also had to suffer the humiliation of his own failed schemes. Immediately after God spoke to him in Genesis 15, he agreed with Sarah to sleep with their maidservant Hagar in hopes of conceiving a child through her. It worked, and Ishmael was born. But this shortsighted attempt to "help God out" backfired and brought sadness and heartache to everyone involved.

God often delays his answers so that we will have plenty of opportunity to fail using our own resources. Only then does God act, but when he does, it demonstrates he alone is responsible for answering our prayers and he alone must get the glory.

3. To deepen our trust in God.

I think that's why Hebrews 11 gives more space to Abraham's story than any other Old Testament hero. *He is the preeminent man of faith in the Bible.* When we read his story and see how long he waited (25 years), we gain a new perspective on our own situation.

If Abraham had to wait, it should not surprise us that we will often have to wait a long time for the fulfillment of our dreams and the answers to our prayers. As with Abraham, waiting is not bad if it causes us to deepen our trust in God and to learn more about his character.

The Answer Is a Person

God's answer to fear is not an argument or a formula. It's a Person. That's why he said to Abraham, "Fear not. I am your shield." God himself is the final answer to every fear of the human heart.

Have you ever wondered why God called himself by the name "I AM" in the Old Testament? Above all else, it means God is eternally existent and therefore all creation depends on him. God stands alone. No one can be compared to him. He is complete in himself. *God doesn't need us, but we desperately need him.*

Think of it this way. To say God is the great "I AM" means that when we come to him, he is everything we need at exactly that moment. It's as if God is saying …

> I am your strength.
> I am your courage.
> I am your health.
> I am your hope.
> I am your supply.
> I am your defender.
> I am your deliverer.
> I am your forgiveness.
> I am your joy.
> I am your future.

God is saying to you and me, "I am whatever you need, whenever you need it." *He is the all-sufficient God for every crisis.*

From Fear to Faith

Let's wrap up this chapter by looking at four principles that will move us from fear to faith.

1. Faith focuses on God, not on our problems.

A woman told me she had changed her phone number and left it unlisted because she is gripped with fear as she thinks about certain people and what they might do to her. As we talked together, I finally said, "It's time to move from fear to faith. Are you ready to move with me?" She smiled hesitantly and then said yes. We prayed, claiming God's promises of protection. When I saw her the next day, she said she had slept much better because she wasn't focusing on her fears.

Think of Abraham. The past argued against his ever having a child. So did the present. His only hope lay in the promises of God for the future. *As long as he looked back, he would never have faith to believe God.* His only hope was to step out into the future, trusting that somehow, someway, God would keep his promises.

2. Faith trusts in God's timing, not your own.

So many of our struggles with fear start right here. *Deep down, we fear God has somehow made a mistake in his dealings with us.* Like Abraham, we have waited and waited—sometimes for years on end. Even though we may have seen many remarkable answers to prayer, the one thing that means the most to us has not been granted.

As I write these words, I am thinking of certain people I know who pray faithfully week after week for their loved ones to be saved. Some of them write notes each week asking prayer for an unsaved husband or wife. Week in and week out the requests come in and the staff prays for them faithfully. One husband has been praying for his wife for many years with no real change in sight. Another wife faithfully requests prayer for her husband. Sometimes he seems interested in spiritual things, and then his interest suddenly seems to disappear.

Where is God? Why doesn't he answer the fervent, heartfelt prayers of his people?

Of the many answers that might be given to that question, one answer must be that God's timing and ours are often quite different. *Sometimes it seems like we live in one time zone and God lives in another.*

3. Faith grows by believing God in spite of your circumstances.

Sometimes our circumstances make it easy to believe in God; other times we have to struggle. As I write these words, I have a friend who is entering the final stages of his battle with cancer. After long and difficult treatments, there is nothing else the doctors can do. He is one of the finest men I know; a man whose gentle spirit endears him to others. No one knows how much time he has left, but it seems to be a matter of a few days. The last time I talked with him, he spoke about the goodness of God. He added he and his wife had had a long and happy life together and they knew God would take care of them. His wife said simply, "No matter what happens, we are trusting in the Lord." That's biblical faith rising above circumstances to lay hold of the eternal promises of God.

4. Faith obeys God one step at a time.

This principle is often overlooked by those seeking to do God's will. God promised a child and Abraham desperately wanted to see the fulfillment of that promise. So what does God tell him to do? Round up the animals for a sacrifice (see Genesis 15:9-11). How do you get from there to the nursery? Abraham doesn't have a clue, and God doesn't tell him a thing. But Abraham now has a choice. He can choose to obey God, round up the animals, and get ready for a sacrifice, even though it doesn't seem to connect with the son of his dreams. Or he can argue with God and decide to take matters in his own hands.

How often we stumble over this. We slight the near in favor of the far, shirking the duties of today because we are dreaming about some distant tomorrow. But until we do what God has called us to do today, we will never be prepared for what he wants us to do tomorrow.

In the end 99 percent of life turns out to be humdrum, ordinary routine. It's the same old thing day after day. *Yet out of the humdrum God is weaving an unseen pattern that will one day lead us in a new direction.* Faith takes the next step— whatever it is—and walks with God wherever he leads. Sometimes it will make sense, other times it won't. But we still must take that step if we are going to do God's will.

Can God Be Trusted?

Everything I've been trying to say comes down to one simple question: Can God be trusted to do what is right? If the answer is yes, then we can face the worst life has to offer. If the answer is no, then we're no better off than the people who have no faith at all. In fact, if the answer is no or if we're not sure, then we really don't have any faith anyway.

As I look to the world around me, many things remain mysterious and unanswerable. But if there is no God, and if he is not good, then nothing at all makes sense. *I have chosen to believe because I must believe.* I have no other choice.

"But I Can Trust"

Pioneer missionary J. Hudson Taylor founded the China Inland Mission in 1865. During the terrible days of the Boxer Rebellion (1899–1901), when missionaries were being captured and killed, he went through such agony of soul that he could not pray. Writing in his journal, he summarized his spiritual condition this way: "I can't read. I can't think. I can't pray. But I can trust."

There will be times when we can't read the Bible. Sometimes we won't be able to focus our thoughts on God at all. *Often we will not even be able to pray.* But in those moments when we can't do anything else, we can still trust in the loving purposes of our heavenly Father.

Fear not, child of God. No one knows what a day may bring. Who knows if we will make it through this week? *But our God is faithful to keep every one of his promises.* Nothing can happen to us unless it first passes through the hands of God. If your way is dark, keep believing. His eye is on the sparrow, and I know he cares for you.

6

QUESTIONS AND ANSWERS

Whenever we go through hard times, we have many questions about God, about good and evil, and about how we can respond to the trials of life. In this chapter we will address some of the common questions asked by those who want to keep on believing in spite of hard times.

Question: Why is there so much suffering and evil in the world?

Answer: This question is both simple and difficult. Or it is easy and impossible. Suffering and evil come as a byproduct of sin in the universe. Romans 5:12 tells us death came into the world as a result of sin. Romans 8:20–22 speaks of all creation being in bondage to decay. In a world without sin, there would be no death, no pain, no suffering, no loss, no senility, no sickness, and no suffering.

God did not create the world with a bent toward its own destruction. Man added that feature all by himself.

Once Adam ate the forbidden fruit, sin entered the human bloodstream, and it has remained there until this very day. From that one act of disobedience has come a river of evil, pain, and death. That river still flows throughout the world, touching everyone born on the planet.

The impossible part of the question deals with the ultimate "Why?" behind sin. Why did God create a universe where Adam's sin could take place? How could God allow such suffering in the world he created? The greatest minds have probed these questions over the centuries. The Christian answer includes these elements: *First*, although God permitted sin, he himself is not morally guilty of sin. *Second*, God will ultimately be glorified through every decision he has made, including the decision to permit sin in the first place. *Third*, God has offered the ultimate solution to the "sin problem" by offering his own Son as the ultimate sacrifice for sin. *Fourth*, giving man free will also meant giving him the freedom to do wrong.

Question: Do you believe in miraculous healing through prayer?

Answer: I believe God can and sometimes does heal through means that seem to be miraculous. The Lord Jesus often worked miracles of healing through his Word and through his touch. No one who reads the Gospels can doubt the mighty power of the Lord. Furthermore, I am not able to find any clear statement in Scripture that indicates God cannot or will not work miracles today when it is according to his will. He can work miracles, and he does when it is according to his divine plan.

Yet not everyone we pray for is healed. Some stay sick for months and others eventually die. Even those who are healed die sooner or later. This is one of those hard facts we must all face sooner or later. Every Christian funeral testifies to the fact that the "last enemy" that will be destroyed is death (see 1 Corinthians 15:26). Like all pastors, I have performed my share of heartbreaking funeral services for believers who died despite the fervent prayers of many people. So whatever else we may say about miraculous healing, it doesn't happen all the time, and it doesn't happen as often as we wish it would. But it does happen. I have seen some cases of dramatic recovery that seemed to be beyond normal medical explanation. While serving in a church in Texas, I was approached by a woman who asked if I would anoint her with oil and pray for her healing. The thought was entirely new to me since the church I grew up in did not do such things, nor had I received any training for this in seminary. But the woman's request was biblical, being based on James 5:14–15:

> Is any one of you sick? He should call the elders of
> the church to pray over him and anoint him with
> oil in the name of the Lord. And the prayer offered
> in faith will make the sick person well; the Lord will
> raise him up. If he has sinned, he will be forgiven.

There are several points worth noting. *First*, the call comes from the sick person who feels the need for prayer. *Second*, the elders are to gather at the sick person's bedside and literally pray "over" him. *Third*, anointing with oil has no curative power in itself but must be done "in the name of the Lord." *Fourth*, God must himself grant the faith to believe the healing will take place. Both the faith and the healing come from the Lord. *Fifth*, the prayer is offered in view of healing without regard to the means. This means the prayer should not be offered as a substitute for medical care but in conjunction with the best medical advice available at the time. *Sixth*, since sickness can sometimes be the result of sin, healing will not come until those sins are honestly confessed and forsaken.

I had not thought through all this when the woman came asking for prayer. Years earlier she had undergone one of the first heart bypass operations. Now her arteries had become like chalk, and she had a severe blockage in her lower abdomen. Because of her frail condition, the doctors were reluctant to operate. Would we pray for a reversal of the blockage?

I will never forget meeting with this dear woman in my office after a Sunday morning service. Several of my elders joined me as she told her story. Not knowing what else to do, I read James 5:14–15, asked her if she had any sins to confess, then I dipped my finger in olive oil and dabbed a bit on her forehead. One by one the elders and I prayed for God to heal her. We were all aware of a powerful sense of God's presence that filled the room.

Two days later she called me with exciting news. Upon returning to her doctor, she was told her blockage had entirely disappeared, and that surgery would not be necessary. We all rejoiced upon hearing the good report. We knew God had answered our prayers.

That was my first experience in praying for the sick according to James 5:14–15. In the years since then I have repeated that simple procedure many different times with many different people suffering from many different ailments. I wish I could tell you that each time I have prayed the person has been healed, but that would not be true. Often I have experienced that same sense of God's presence, and often individuals have reported improvement in their conditions. But those reports have generally come when prayer has been combined with compassionate medical treatment.

Sometimes I have prayed for dear friends to be healed from cancer and other diseases only to discover I would later officiate at their funerals. I suppose every pastor could say the same thing.

One other note: I hadn't heard a thing about the woman we prayed for until I heard she had died of congestive heart failure some years later. So even though I believe she was healed in answer to prayer, she eventually died because death is still "the last enemy" of the people of God.

Whenever anyone asks my theology of healing, I tell them very simply, "We do the praying and God does the healing—in his own time, in his own way, according to his own will."

Question: What happens when we die?

Answer: It depends on what happens before you die. Those who have trusted Jesus Christ as Savior go immediately into the presence of the Lord. They are "away from the body and at home with the Lord" (2 Corinthians 5:8). As the apostle Paul languished in a Roman jail, he expressed a desire to depart from his earthly body and to be with Christ in heaven. In his mind, dying would be gain because it would usher him into the personal presence of Jesus Christ (Philippians 1:21–23). Jesus made the same promise to the thief on the cross: "Today you will be with me in paradise" (Luke 23:43).

Meanwhile the body is buried awaiting the day of resurrection. First Thessalonians 4:13-18 tells us that when Jesus returns to the earth the "dead in Christ" will rise first. That means there will be a literal resurrection of the bodies of believers who died "in Christ." That resurrection will be no less literal and no less physical than Jesus' own resurrection.

Often while conducting a graveside service, I will remind those present of the words Moses said when he heard the voice coming from the burning bush: "Take off your sandals, for the place where you are standing is holy ground" (Exodus 3:5). Then I will say something like this: "This place of burial is holy ground. Look around you. Today all you see are signs of death. Gravestones, markers, flowers, monuments. Everything about this place is quiet, peaceful, serene. It is a good place to bury the dead. But it won't always be like this. When Jesus returns, this very spot will be a place of resurrection. Take off your shoes, you are standing on resurrection ground."

But what happens to those who die without Jesus Christ? They are sent immediately into a place of torment called hell. They will remain there until the Great White Throne judgment when they will be condemned for all eternity and cast into the lake of fire (Luke 16:19–31; Revelation 20:11–15).

If these things are true, then the most important decision you can ever make is the decision to trust Jesus Christ as Lord and Savior.

And the most important thing you can ever do for your friends and loved ones is to share the good news that Jesus died and rose again and wants to be their Savior.

Question: How can I overcome my fear of death?

Answer: First of all, you have nothing to be ashamed of. Millions of people share your fear of death and dying. Sometimes the fear of dying has more to do with the possible pain and suffering associated with death. It is certainly true you may die in a way that is unpleasant or even painful. Most of us won't be able to orchestrate the time and place of our own death, and we won't be able to control the circumstances.

At this point we are faced once again with the central question of this book: Do we believe God is in control and that he is good and has our best interests at heart? If God is in control, then we may rest assured that he has numbered our days from the beginning to the end and that our life rests safely in his hands. That doesn't mean we are immune to sudden death, cancer, or a lingering, painful death. But it does mean we don't have to live in abject fear of those things. Hebrews 2:15 tells us that Jesus came to "free those who all their lives were held in slavery by their fear of death." Because he died and rose from the dead, Jesus can set us free from overwhelming fear.

One of my college professors mentioned in class that her aunt was at the point of death and was struggling with her feelings of fear and personal failure. I remember the professor said she was praying that God would give her aunt "dying grace." The term perfectly describes one special ministry of the Holy Spirit. I believe he can give the children of God special comfort and a sense of abiding peace in the last hours of life on earth. Someone once asked John Wesley what made his followers so different from others. "Our people die well," he replied. Indeed, Christians of all people ought to "die well," for we have the assurance of eternal life through Jesus Christ. And that thought brings us full circle back to your question. Do you know Jesus Christ as Lord and Savior? Have you ever committed yourself to him without reservation? If the answer is no or if you are not sure, I urge you to place your trust in him without delay. God's answer to your fear of death is his Son who conquered death on your behalf.

Question: I've gone through many trials lately. How can I discover what God is saying to me through these hard times?

Answer: Often we won't be able to discern any particular message from a particular trial while we are going through it. Sometimes we won't see a purpose for our hardships until they are through and we can look back and see God's hand at work. Sometimes even then the things we have endured will make no sense.

In those cases we must go back to the words of Scripture. Job 23:10 tells us, "But he knows the way that I take; when he has tested me, I will come forth as gold." The first part of the verse is the key to the second part. God knows what you are going through right now. He sees it and knows, for before the beginning of time he ordained this trial for you. It has not happened to you by "chance" or "luck" or "fate" or "cruel misfortune." Do not fall into the trap of believing those worldly explanations. The old expression "Into each life some rain must fall" reveals an important truth. No one gets an easy road to heaven. Though the price of entry has been paid with the blood of Christ, the road we must travel on earth is filled with "many dangers, toils, and snares."

Therefore, we must not be surprised when a multitude of "fiery trials" come our way, sometimes one after another and sometimes two or three at the same time. God sends trials as part of his plan to bring us to maturity, to conform us to the image of Christ, and to cause us to "come forth as gold."

Many years ago I worked in a factory that produced soft-drink bottles. Once the molten glass was forced into the mold, a perfectly shaped bottle emerged and began traveling down the assembly line. It immediately went into an oven, which baked the bottle at an extremely high temperature for about ten minutes. One night I saw the foreman take a newly molded bottle from the assembly line before it had gone into the oven. When he poured water on it, the bottle shattered. He explained that unless the bottle had been "tempered" by the hot oven, it would shatter under the slightest pressure. But once tempered, it could withstand high-pressure bottling.

The same is true for you and me. The trials of life "temper" us and make us stronger. As painful as they are, these trials are actually gifts from God, even though we never think so when we are in the middle of a hard time.

The truth is, you will often not know why God sends a particular trial at a particular time, but you can rest assured God makes no mistakes and in the end will produce gold in your life.

Question: The son of my best friend recently died in an automobile accident. Now she blames herself for his death, even though she had nothing to do with the accident. How can I help my friend through this crisis?

Answer: The very best thing you can do is simply to be there for her. Proverbs 17:17 says, "A friend loves at all times, and a brother is born for adversity." Your friend will never forget that you cared enough to spend time with her during her darkest days. Remember, too, that Job's friends helped him more during the seven days they were silent than when they finally started talking. It's OK not to have all the answers. Assure your friend that you love her and that God loves her. As you have the opportunity, gently remind her that God will not hold her responsible for her son's death. Point her toward the cross, where God's own Son died for the sins of the world. She needs to know that God knows what she is going through. He's been there because he watched his Son die on a bloody Roman cross—and that was no accident, but the treacherous act of sinful men.

Finally, give your friend the time and space she needs to go through the grieving process. Her life will never be the same, and she will need your friendship more now than ever before.

Question: Although I was raised in the church as a child, somewhere along the way I lost my faith. I am trying to find something to believe in but don't know where to begin. Can you help me?

Answer: I am happy to tell you that you are in excellent shape for a new beginning. The first step in changing your life is to admit that things really do need to change. Your story reminds me of so many people who were raised in Christian homes, but somewhere along the way they drifted away from the Lord and from the church.

Sometimes we make our quest for faith too difficult. Jesus instructed us to have the faith of a child if we truly want to know God. "I tell you the truth, unless you change and become like little children, you will never enter the kingdom of heaven" (Matthew 18:3). Think of the faith of a child. What words come to mind? Innocence, simplicity, humility, honesty. Above all else, a little child has a trusting heart. He believes because no one has given him a reason not to believe.

You once had that kind of faith but now it has disappeared. May I recommend three simple steps? *First, go back to the Bible and begin reading it again.* It doesn't really matter where you begin, but each day set aside a few minutes to let God speak to you personally through his Word. *Second, begin each day with this prayer:* "Lord Jesus, I come to you as a little child. Help me to grow in my faith as I walk with you today. Amen." *Third, tell at least three people this week that you are on a journey to rediscover your faith in God.* Sharing that fact will strengthen your resolve and it may also challenge them to do the same.

Finally, don't feel like you have to have all your questions answered. Come to Christ with childlike confidence, and he will give you the faith to believe again.

Question: I feel like a failure. Recently I lost my job when the company decided they no longer needed my services. They said it was nothing personal, but I feel like a loser anyway. What do I do now?

Answer: Don't give up. You're not the first person to lose your job. And you're not the first person ever to feel like a failure. If we're honest, all of us have experienced failure. We've all been rejected, passed over, flunked out, cut from the team, or otherwise made to feel we somehow aren't needed or wanted. Failure is simply a part of life, and the longer we live, the more opportunity we have to fail.

Failure is the most democratic of all clubs, admitting old and young, rich and poor, men and women. About the only thing its members have in common is their secrecy about belonging. Think what a national convention of all eligible members of the Failure Club would look like—millions of people crowded tightly together in thousands of rooms across America, all looking down at their feet.

I have three pieces of good news for you. *First, the Bible records the stories of many abysmal failures.* Abraham lied about his wife, Moses killed a man, David committed adultery, and Peter denied Christ. These were some of the greatest men in the Bible, yet their failures are recorded for all the world to see.

Second, God specializes in helping failures find a new start in life. After all, that's what salvation is all about. Until you admit you are a failure, you can never be saved. In that sense we're all failures because all of us have sinned against a holy God. Since only sinners can be saved, the only people in heaven will be those with the courage to admit they failed while on the earth.

One final thought: *God expects more failure from you than you expect from yourself.* God knows we're going to fail, and he is not surprised when we do. This is very freeing, for it means he still loves us and cares for us. Our acceptance is not based upon our performance.

When Jesus told Peter, "Follow me!" (John 21:19), he was showing him the way back from failure and defeat. Remember, he knows you're going to fail. When it comes right down to it, the important thing is whether you are going to follow him. Jesus can help restore your hope, and he can give you the desire to get back up if you will follow him. Jesus never failed, but he loves failures like you and me.

7

A FRIEND IN HIGH PLACES

Do you have clout?
    The answer is, it depends on who you know. That's how Mike Royko explained the meaning of the word.

For over 30 years Mike Royko was the voice of Chicago to the nation. At the height of his career over 600 newspapers carried his columns. After he died in 1997, his family and friends published 110 of his columns (out of almost 8,000 he wrote) in a bestselling book called *One More Time*.

A column from 1967 discusses the proper meaning of the word "clout." It seems that someone sent him a copy of *Vogue* magazine that included a survey of people with "clout." The list included President Lyndon Johnson, Ho Chi Minh, and the Pope. Royko called it "a surprisingly dumb thing to write. And they have a lot of nerve stealing an old Chicago word and distorting its meaning" (p. 17).

Everyone from Chicago knows what clout is. Clout makes the city tick. *Royko's point is that clout never goes down, it always goes up.* Clout is what you have if you can call city hall and make a parking ticket disappear. Clout is what you have if you can get a private meeting with the governor. Or to use Royko's examples, a Chicago police officer might have enough clout with a ward boss to get a promotion to sergeant. The ward boss might have enough clout with the mayor to get a sweetheart contract for his brother-in-law. And the mayor might have enough clout with the White House to get an extra $10 million in pork barrel money for the city. That's clout. It's a grand old Chicago word.

If you've got clout, it means you've got a friend in high places. *We all understand that because we all need help from time to time.* Maybe we can't get a job interview, or we can't get in to see the doctor, or we need some help at city hall. We need someone who can cut through the red tape and help us when we can't help ourselves.

Hebrews 4:14–16 tells us that Jesus is the friend we need. We love to sing "What a friend we have in Jesus," but is there anything to those words at all? Our text gives us the answer. Jesus is the friend we need because he is the Right Person with the Right Past in the Right Place.

To use Mike Royko's word, we've got clout in heaven.

The Right Person

"Therefore, since we have a great high priest who has gone through the heavens, Jesus the Son of God, let us hold firmly to the faith we profess" (Hebrews 4:14).

Most of us are at a disadvantage when we read this verse because we don't have a clear notion of what a high priest is. The main thing we need to know is that the high priest was the number one person in the Old Testament religious system. There were various levels and orders of priests in Judaism, but there was only one high priest. His chief job was to represent the nation of Israel on the Day of Atonement. On that day he would go behind the thick veil that separated the Holy Place from the Most Holy Place. There he would offer the blood of a goat on the golden Mercy Seat that sat atop the Ark of the Covenant. When the blood was offered in the way God prescribed, the sins of the people were atoned or covered for another year (see Leviticus 16).

That system was never meant to last forever. The high priest had to repeat the sacrifice year after year. When one high priest died, he was replaced by another who continued the yearly sacrifice on the Day of Atonement. Now that Christ has come, the sacrificial system of the Old Testament has been abolished. Christ has become our great high priest who has passed through the heavens into the sanctuary of God. *Unlike the sacrifices of the Old Testament high priests, Christ's sacrifice never needs to be repeated.* Through his death on the cross, he made a complete and final atonement for our sins.

He is the right person to hear our prayers because he has entered the Holy of Holies in heaven. He is Jesus (his human name), and he is also the Son of God (his divine title). The same Jesus who once walked on the earth is now in heaven, having opened the way to God by his own eternal sacrifice.

The Right Past

"For we do not have a high priest who is unable to sympathize with our weaknesses, but we have one who has been tempted in every way, just as we are—yet was without sin" (Hebrews 4:15).

The King James Version says that Jesus is "touched with the feeling of our infirmities." He is "touched" by the weakness of our feeble flesh. Whatever touches us, touches him. To say "I feel your pain" has become a cliché today, but in Jesus' case it is true. *He is moved by our sorrow, aware of our tears, and touched by our failure.*

Sometimes when we are in the middle of a hard time, well-meaning people will say, "I know what you are going through." In my opinion that is often a cruel thing to say. How can you be sure you know what another person is thinking or feeling? I think it's better not to say that because if you really do know what another person is going through, your heart will make that clear to them. And if you don't, it's far better not to say anything at all.

As I thought about this, my mind drifted back to something that happened 45 years ago. During my growing up years in a small Alabama town, one of my good friends was Hal Kirby, Jr. We used to wrestle in his front yard and then we would go inside his house and watch television. In my mind's eye I can still see the room where we played games and read comic books by the hour. When we were in the seventh grade, Hal went on a trip on the Natchez Trace with our youth group. When he came home that evening, he was sick. The next day he died suddenly. It was the first time I had ever been that close to death.

Now fast-forward almost 10 years. In November 1974 my father died after a brief illness. Because he was a beloved physician, it seemed as if everyone in town came to pay their respects. People I didn't know told me stories about my father. Men and women wept openly at the funeral home. After all these years the events surrounding my father's death are a blur in my memory. I recall hundreds of people stopping by to express their sympathy, but I don't remember what anyone said. Except for one person. The scene is etched clearly in my mind, although it could not have lasted more than 20 seconds. I was sitting in a bedroom at home talking with some friends. In came Hal Kirby, Sr. He put his arm on my shoulder and said, "Ray, we're so sorry to hear about your father. He was a good man. If there is anything we can do, let us know." That was it. A few words and he was gone. But what a message those few words conveyed. Because I knew he knew what it meant to lose someone you love, his words are the only ones that have stayed with me in the years since my father died.

That's what our text means when it says Jesus is touched with the feeling of our infirmities. He knows our pain, he sees our weakness, he understands what we are going through. Because he was a "man of sorrows and acquainted with grief," he is qualified to help us when life falls apart.

C. S. Lewis on Temptation

How good it is to know he was tempted just as we are. The text means Jesus faced every kind of temptation we can face. Every temptation falls into one of three categories: the lust of the eyes, the lust of the flesh, and the pride of life (cf. 1 John 2:14–17).

Jesus defeated the devil in those three areas. Where we failed, he succeeded. Where we gave in, he stood strong. Where we collapsed under pressure, Jesus obeyed his Father. He was tempted, yet he never sinned by giving in. I find great comfort in these words of C. S. Lewis in his book *Mere Christianity*:

> A silly idea is current that good people do not know what temptation means. This is an obvious lie. Only those who try to resist temptation know how strong it is. After all, you find out the strength of the German army by fighting against it, not by giving in. You find out the strength of a wind by trying to walk against it, not by lying down. A man who gives in to temptation after five minutes simply does not know what it would have been like an hour later. That is why bad people, in one sense, know very little about badness. They have lived a sheltered life by always giving in ... Christ, because He was the only man who never yielded to temptation, is also the only man who knows to the full what temptation means (p. 142).

This has enormous implications for our spiritual life. *Because Christ was tempted and never gave in, we may be sure he is never surprised by anything we say or do.* We gave in too early, so we never felt the full force of temptation. But Jesus let the waves of temptation rush over him and stood like the Rock of Gibraltar. When we pray, we don't have to worry that we will somehow shock him. He's heard it all and seen it all. We can go ahead and be totally honest about our failures. He knows about it even before we tell him.

Ron Dunn and Jesus

And we don't have to prove ourselves worthy when we pray. I take great encouragement from something Ron Dunn wrote in a

book called *Don't Just Stand There, Pray Something!* He tells what he
learned at the end of a very bad day. When he woke up, he didn't
spend time praying. As the day wore on, he was churlish in the way
he treated people. When the day finally ended, he knelt to pray and
began by saying, "Lord, I've made a mess of my life today, and I
confess I'm not worthy to come into your presence." At that point
he felt the Lord interrupt his prayer. "Ron, do you think having a
quiet time this morning would have made you worthy to talk to
me? Do you think doing good and treating people right would have
somehow made you qualified to come into my presence? If that's
what you think, you don't know yourself, you don't know me, and
you don't understand the grace of God." I can relate to that story
because most of the time that's exactly how I think. It's so easy for
us to believe our good works somehow commend us to God, that if
we'll just "be good," God is more likely to hear our prayers.

But to think like that is to deny the gospel itself. *We are accepted
by God only on the basis of what Jesus Christ has done.* How dare we
wave the tattered rags of a quiet time and think that somehow that
makes a difference in heaven. I'm all for having a quiet time and
all for treating people right and totally on the side of living for the
Lord, but all of that cannot add even a tiny sliver to our acceptance
before God. It is either all by grace or not by grace at all.

Because Jesus knows how sinful we really are, we don't have to
play games when we pray. We can come to God just the way we
are, clinging only to the cross and claiming nothing but the blood
of Jesus as our only hope of being accepted when we pray.

Our text contains one final truth that should encourage us when
we pray. Jesus is not only the Right Person with the Right Past, but
he is also in the Right Place to give us the help we need.

The Right Place

"Let us then approach the throne of grace with confidence, so
that we may receive mercy and find grace to help us in our time of
need" (Hebrews 4:16).

When we pray, we are invited to come to the "throne of grace." Because of Jesus, the throne of God's justice is now a throne of grace. When we come before that throne, we will not be turned away. Many people think God's throne is like the principal's office in high school. Do you remember what it was like to be called to the principal's office? Nothing good could happen behind that closed door. You were bound to get in trouble if you went in there. That's how many of us think of God's throne because we have a vision of an angry God who is looking for a chance to hurl a lightning bolt at us. But it is not true. *When we come to God in Jesus' name, he's glad to see us.* He knows who we are, he calls us by name, and he welcomes us before the throne. "My child," he says, "what can I do for you today?"

That's why we are to come with confidence or boldness. *When we come before God in prayer, we don't have to be ashamed or act bashful or watch our words lest we say something wrong.* We can unburden our heart before the Lord and say whatever we want to say. A friend showed me a card he received from the National Hockey League that admits him free of charge to every arena in the NHL. All he has to do is show the card and he gets free VIP parking, free admittance to the special entrance for players and management, and the right to enter otherwise restricted areas. The card gets him in free and gives him special privileges, but it does him no good unless he uses it. If he wants to, he can still pay for parking and still pay for his ticket and still sit with the general public. The card has to be used boldly to do him any good. Otherwise the privileges that are his will go unused. *God has given to every Christian a card that says, "Admit to the Throne Room of Heaven."* The card is stamped with the blood of Jesus Christ. But that card does you no good unless you use it boldly when you pray.

"Lord, Have Mercy"

Mercy is what gets us out of trouble.
Grace gives us what we don't deserve.

A friend gave me a tape of a speech Gary Olson made to a group of Christian coaches. Gary was a former elder of our church in Oak Park, Illinois, and for many years was the head football coach at Oak Park-River Forest High School. He talked to the coaches about how to handle the hard times of life. He told them how he collapsed during football practice and was taken to the hospital where the doctors discovered he had an enlarged heart. A few days later he had surgery to replace a defective heart valve. Not long after that his mother suddenly died of a brain hemorrhage. It seemed almost too much to bear. He said he called his pastor and asked, "How should I pray?" His pastor told him to pray "Lord, have mercy. God, have mercy. Jesus, have mercy." I was his pastor and also a very good friend. I smiled when I heard him tell the story because I had forgotten that phone call. Then it all came back to me. I gave my answer off the top of my head, but it was perfectly biblical.

There are many times in life when the only thing we can do is to cry out, "God, have mercy. Lord, have mercy. Jesus, have mercy." When we pray like that, we will find the mercy we need from God.

Verse 16 ends with the good news that we can find grace whenever we need it. One translation says we can find "grace to help in the nick of time." I like that. The last phrase literally means "at the right moment." *God's answers are always perfectly timed.* Not too soon and not too late. And often they do seem to come "in the nick of time." God gives us the grace we need, but not until we truly need it.

It's a liberating thing to feel complete freedom to come into God's presence. One of our sons helped me understand this years ago during an all-night prayer meeting. We began every hour that night with a brief devotional by a different person. During the hour assigned to me, I gave a brief devotional and then we spent the remainder of the hour in prayer. After I finished speaking, a friend said to me, "Did you see what Josh did?" Our oldest son was probably 5 years old at the time. "What did he do?" I hadn't noticed anything. My friend said, "While you were talking to us, Josh came up to you and asked a question. You stopped your talk, leaned over, and answered him.

Then you finished your talk." I didn't even remember the incident because it happened so naturally. Because he was my son, Josh knew he could come to me anytime, even when I was speaking, and I would not turn him away. That's the "boldness" and "freedom of speech" that all of us ought to have when we pray.

I come now to the bottom line, and it is good news for all of us. We've got a friend in high places. In the words of Mike Royko, we've got clout. *We've got connections in heaven.* We've got a friend at the throne of grace who delights to answer our prayers because he's the Right Person with the Right Past in the Right Place. Because he feels your pain, he can sympathize with what you're going through. Nothing you say will surprise him.

Come boldly. Come often. Come to the throne of grace and pour out your heart to God. You will not be turned away.

8

IF GOD IS GOOD, WHY DO I HURT?

Of all the questions that trouble the people of God, none is greater than the question posed in the title of this chapter. Sometimes it is asked in other ways: Why is there so much suffering in the world? Or why do bad things happen to good people? Or why do the wicked prosper while the righteous take a beating? Or if God really has the power to stop human suffering, why doesn't he use it?

Eventually these questions become very personal: Why did I lose my job? Why did God allow my daughter to die in a car wreck? If God is good, how could he let my closest friend suddenly have a heart attack? There is no end to the questions, and there is an alarming shortage of satisfying answers. No question for a pastor is harder to answer than, "Why did this happen?" I rest content that at best I can grasp a tiny sliver of God's eternal purposes as they work themselves out in a fallen world where death still reigns.

The Keyhole Principle

We rarely grasp all that God is doing in any particular situation. As John Piper puts it, God is doing 10,000 things in your life right now. You understand maybe 3 of those things. Said another way, we can't even imagine all the different ways God is working all things for our own good and his glory. Or we can put it this way: We don't know what we don't know.

We are like little children peering through a keyhole. *We see a tiny bit, but the rest is hidden from our view.* The danger comes in assuming that our "keyhole view" equals the totality of God's purposes.

What can we learn from this?

1. We won't understand most things that happen to us or to our loved ones.
2. The understanding we do have will be partial and limited.
3. Some things will baffle us completely.
4. If we get stuck on "understanding" everything, we are bound to be extremely frustrated.
5. Every now and then things will make perfect sense to us. When that happens, we ought to be grateful and even then remember that when we think we know the big picture, we're still looking through the keyhole of life.

This truth ought to *build our faith* ("God is at work in my life in 10,000 different ways right now") and it ought *to humble us* ("I'm not smart enough to figure out all that God is doing in any particular situation") and it ought *to give us hope* ("God knows what he is doing, even when my current situation makes no sense to me").

Let me make this personal. Why am I alive while someone else suddenly dies? I faced that question when the pastor of a large church in Chicago died suddenly. At the time I served as pastor of Calvary Memorial Church; he was the pastor of Calvary Church in another Chicago suburb. The next day someone told me that he had heard the pastor's death announced on a local radio station, but he only heard the part where the announcer said the pastor of Calvary Church had died suddenly. He assumed they were talking about me. And the thought comes—it could have been me. Why the other pastor and not me? Only God knows the answer.

The question before us focuses on the connection between God's goodness and our pain. In thinking about where to turn in the Bible to find help on this topic, my mind was drawn to a simple statement in the Book of Job where the afflicted saint declares his faith in God. His words have endured across the centuries because they speak for everyone who has spent some time in the furnace of suffering. Some people are in the furnace right now, others have just come out, and the rest of us will be there sooner or later.

Three Truths for Those in the Furnace

Here is Job's simple statement that sums up an enormous spiritual truth: "He knows the way that I take; when he has tested me, I will come forth as gold" (Job 23:10). Let's focus on three important truths that if properly understood will help you hang on to your faith while living in the furnace.

Truth # 1: God knows what you are going through.

Job begins by affirming his confidence that God sees him in his pain: *"He knows the way that I take."* Nothing matters more than this when life throws us a curveball. Not long ago I managed to mangle my ankle in a biking accident. It happened when I hit an ice patch, and my bicycle slid out from under me. I ended up with three broken bones and a dislocated left ankle. That led to three surgeries and many months of recovery and rehab. While I was awaiting my first surgery, I was thinking about that congregational response that goes "God is good, all the time, and all the time, God is good." A few years ago, I mentioned in a sermon that it started in the churches of Nigeria. A woman in Nigeria wrote to say it's true that they say that in their churches. Then she said that the congregation adds a line at the end: "I am a witness." I heard about a church that added two other phrases to that antiphonal chant: "In every situation" and "no matter what." You could combine it all this way:

"God is good."
"All the time."
"In every situation."
"No matter what."
"I am a witness."

If you want to remember it, hold up your hand and say those phrases, touching a different finger each time. It's a good way to tattoo the truth on your soul.

While waiting for surgery, I found my emotions going in all directions at once. So I kept reminding myself of the first phrase of Job 23:10, "He knows the way that I take."

He knew all about the ice.
He knew the path I would ride.
He knew that I would fall.

Nothing was hidden from him. As I kept repeating that truth, it steadied my heart. I can join with believers around the world and say not only that "God is good" but "I am a witness."

Let's make this personal to your situation. Whatever you are going through right now, God knows all about it. He knows about your divorce, he knows about your cancer, he knows how your kids are struggling, he knows you are running out of money, he knows how you struggle with discouragement. Our God knows the path you take. Nothing is hidden from him.

He knows what will happen around the next corner because he is already there. He knows what's going to happen next week. He knows! Aren't you glad God knows every detail of your life, including the parts that seem to be spinning out of control and make no sense at all?

Truth # 2: Spiritual growth is a journey, not a destination.

Notice how Job puts it—"When <u>he</u> has tested me." I've underlined the word <u>he</u> to emphasize that Job understood that God was behind his sufferings. You may say that it was all Satan's doing, but that's not the whole truth. It was God who brought up Job's name in the first place when he asked, "Have you considered my servant Job?" (Job 1:8). And it was God who set the limits on how far Satan could go in tormenting Job. That's why Job kept saying, "I want to talk to God face-to-face about all this." Satan may have started it, but God set the rules of the game.

"When he has tested me." This speaks to the fact that suffering is part of God's process to bring us to spiritual maturity. Write it down in big letters: *We all must go through the furnace sooner or later.* "But it's hot." You're right about that. "It hurts." It sure does. "It seems to last forever." That's how it feels in the furnace. "I don't like it in there." Neither do I. But none of those objections matter in the end.

Warren Wiersbe offers this encouraging word:

> When God puts his own people into the furnace,
> he keeps his eye on the clock and his hand on the
> thermostat. He knows how long and how much.

A friend wrote me a note describing several traumatic events of the last two years, including the death of a parent and a very painful divorce. He said that he was glad to see a new year begin because the last one had been filled with so much pain. The whole year he had been living on the brink. But that's not bad, he said, because out on the jagged edge of life he discovered the grace of God. "I have learned I am a person desperately in need of grace," he added. Hard times are a gift from God to help him see how much he needs the Lord. His pain has taught him that he is like a helpless baby, totally dependent on the Lord.

On one level we all know that's true. It's just that we forget it until life falls apart.

Truth # 3: Your trials have a divine benefit.

The text says, "I will come forth as gold." When you are "in the furnace," it is hard to believe that any good could result from the fiery trial, but God says, "Wait for a while, and you will see pure gold." *During the worst moments, we take this by faith and hang on to God, believing that better days must eventually come.* Thus it is that Job lost everything, Joseph was cast into prison on a phony rape charge, and Jonah ended up in the belly of a great fish. Jonah was a very reluctant prophet whose final words are both angry and accusing. But still he was God's man for Nineveh. God said, "I'm going to send you into the belly of a fish so you can think about things for a while." He did, and eventually he was puked out on the beach (not a very pleasant experience). Job lost everything and gained back more than he lost. Joseph ended up the second most powerful man in Egypt. *Sometimes our trials lead to a promotion; other times we feel like we've been puked up on the beach.* God does it both ways, and we'll probably experience both if we live long enough. But God had bigger things in mind in all three cases. He wasn't through with Job or Joseph or Jonah. Nor is he through with us just because we go through hard times.

After my bike mishap that sent me to the hospital, Harry Bollback told me not to call it an accident. "It's not an accident," he said. "It's an incident." *There are no accidents for the people of God, only incidents.* He's right, and I believe God was in control of every detail that day. Frankly, I'm not very good at sitting and stopping and waiting. But the Lord knew this was what I needed. He blew the whistle and called a timeout just as I crossed that patch of ice.

While reading a book of Puritan prayers, I ran across a statement that said our trials are sent by God for our spiritual improvement. For some reason that struck me with great force. When God wants to improve a person spiritually, he puts him in the furnace.

Job compared it to the process of refining gold. Even though this took place thousands of years ago, the basic process has hardly changed. You take raw chunks of gold ore—pieces of stone flecked with tiny bits of gold—and put them in a hot furnace. The heat causes the stone and dirt to melt and rise to the surface where they are skimmed off, so the only thing left is pure gold. It takes enormous heat to do this, but it's worth it because in the end you have pure gold, unmixed with any impurities.

Something like that is at work in your life through the trials you endure. The hotter the fire, the more the pain, but the quicker the gold comes forth. In the end you will be both approved and improved by God. Your trials are not wasted nor are they random acts of fate.

- You will be *approved*—found to be good.
- You will be *improved*—made to be better.

This may not seem very comforting when you are in the furnace. Even to promise that it won't last forever may seem empty when you feel alone with your troubles. I can't tell you when your trials will end, but I do know this much: He's an on-time God. You can't rush him, but he's never late either. When the appointed time has come, you will come out of the furnace, and the gold of tested character will come forth in your life.

But what about those people whose trials never end in this life? I have known some very fine people whose lives have seemed to be one heartbreak after another. When I see such a person, I never think, "They must be very sinful." Instead, I think to myself, "There must be a lot of gold there."

Here's another piece of good news. For those who know Jesus Christ, death is the end of all suffering. I ran across a marvelous statement of this truth: "God has an eternity to set right what has gone wrong." That's why the apostle Paul could say that our trials aren't worthy to be compared to the glory that will be revealed in us (Romans 8:18). Whether you live or die, if you are a Christian, your trials will not last forever.

Faith = A Moment-by-Moment Choice

So how will we survive the furnace? Very simply, we must consciously choose to believe God in spite of our circumstances. That's what Job did. Here is a man in dire straits—in worse shape than most of us will ever be—and in the midst of his pain he makes a bold declaration: "I'm still serving the Lord. As bad as it's been, nothing can cause me to turn away from God." I ask one simple question: Where does that kind of faith come from? To me, that's a crucial question because as I study my own heart, I'm not so sure that I would be as strong as Job under those circumstances. How does a person stay strong when life tumbles in around him? People who survive great trials understand that faith is a conscious moment-by-moment choice. More specifically, they also understand that faith is not based on how you feel at any given moment.

For years I tended to view faith as an emotion—if I felt good, if things were going well, if I found myself in a powerful worship service, then faith was easy for me. There's only one problem with that concept—it won't work when you don't feel good or things aren't going well or your friends have turned against you or the preacher is boring. Feeling-based faith won't cut it when life crashes in on every side.

In those moments of desperation, you've got a choice to make. It's exactly the same one Job made. He said, "My feet have followed his steps" and "I have not turned aside." I'm sure Job didn't feel like following God after all the tragedies he had endured. But he did it anyway. That's why he survived—and that's why we still talk about him today.

I have a friend who has been battling cancer for several years. Right now the cancer is in remission, but the doctors have said it could return again. Many people have prayed for his complete healing. When I chatted with him on the phone, he said he'd been pondering his own situation from a new perspective. Which is the greater miracle, he wondered, to be healed from cancer or to be given the grace to stay faithful even if he isn't healed completely?

Faith comes in many different varieties, but the faith that wins in the end is faith that chooses to obey God in spite of the outward circumstances.

Changing Our Agenda

Several years ago I read the biography of Bob Pierce, founder of World Vision, the Christian relief organization that has helped millions of people around the world. As I read his story, it struck me that he was an unlikely man to found and lead such a large organization. He didn't have much education, he butchered the "King's English," and he lacked many social graces. In fact, he called himself a second-rater. When asked the secret of his life, he said that in his early years as a Christian he had prayed, "O God, I give you the right to set the agenda for my life. From here on out, you're going to run the show. And you can change that agenda anytime you want. But I pray that you will be pleased to use me for your glory in any way you see fit. Amen."

That's the kind of prayer God can answer because it's based on the truth that God is God and he has the absolute right to do whatever he wants. Many of us are unhappy because we're fighting God at the point of his sovereignty. We've never surrendered our agenda to his control.

To borrow a common phrase, we must "let God be God." On one level that statement is nonsense because God is God whether we like it or not. But on another level it points to a great truth. We can either live in submission to the sovereignty of a God whose ways are far beyond all human understanding, or we can attempt to fight against his plan. But as the wise man said: Your arms are too short to box with God.

Let's sum up the application of this chapter with three simple statements:

Your struggles are necessary—fight on!
Your Father has not forgotten you—hang on!
Your future is assured—walk on!

Here are three good mottoes for life in the furnace: Fight on! Hang on! Walk on!

Above all, don't take matters into your own hands. That only makes things worse. God has important things to teach you in the furnace if only you will listen and learn. We'll all do some "furnace time" because that's part of God's plan for our spiritual growth. You can't escape the furnace, but you can use it for your own spiritual improvement.

Is God Good?

And that brings me back to the original question: If God is good, why do I hurt? I think the first part of that question is the key. Is God really good? More and more I am convinced that this is the fundamental question of life: "Is God good and can he be trusted to do what is right?" If the answer is yes, then we can face the worst that life has to offer. If the answer is no, then we're no better off than the people who have no faith at all. In fact, if the answer is no or if we're not sure, then we really don't have any faith at all.

Sometimes you choose to believe because of what you see; often you believe in spite of what you see. As I look at the world around me, many things remain mysterious and unanswerable. But if there is no God, or if he is not good, then nothing at all makes sense.

If you are hurting as you read these words, you may feel you have come to the end of your endurance. But don't let your feelings determine your faith. *God is always at work whether we see him or not.* I may not "feel" God's presence during some difficult trial. But he's at work in my life with or without my conscious understanding.

He's at work when I see his hand clearly.
He's at work when all is gray and mysterious.

Remember the Keyhole Principle.
You only see a tiny part of the big picture.

You don't understand because you don't need to understand.
When you need to know, you'll know.

Right now we see through a glass darkly.
Better days are coming when all will be made plain.

God knows what he's doing even when we don't.
He's never clueless even when we don't have a clue.

If your way is dark, hang on to Jesus. When your furnace time is over, you will come forth as gold.

9

IF I BELIEVE, WHY DO I DOUBT?

L et's talk about doubt.

It seems strange to say it that way because we rarely talk about doubt in the church. You don't hear many sermons about doubt. It is an unfamiliar topic to most people, even though there are whole books of the Bible that deal with the issue of doubt in various ways, such as Job, Ecclesiastes, Lamentations, and Habakkuk. Many of the Psalms touch on the theme of doubt and feeling abandoned by God.

> We need this message because doubt is a hidden issue inside the church.
> We need this message because sometimes it's not easy to believe.
> We need this message because you may feel disqualified by your doubts.

I received an email from a soldier serving in Afghanistan who had been there since the beginning of the war. Over the years he saw a lot of combat, and it took a toll on his faith. Here is part of what he wrote to me:

I've been in the service since the start of the war, and it is getting emotionally taxing, being at risk so much with a family back home. To be honest, there are days when I doubt the existence of God even though I have grown up in the church … I have struggled to find lasting peace … I had it for a few weeks, but I can see it slipping some.

During my pastorate in Oak Park, Illinois, the young singles group invited me once a year to an "Ask Pastor Ray" night. That was always fun because the group was lively, and they peppered me with unpredictable questions. The last time we met, 50–60 of us sat in a big circle in the church dining room. I told them I would be glad to answer questions about the Bible, the Christian life, theological issues, or they could ask about my personal life. No topic was off-limits. Near the end of the evening, a young lady raised her hand and asked, "Pastor Ray, when I listen to you speak, you always sound so certain about everything. Do you ever doubt?" My answer was short and simple: Yes, I do have doubts. *I don't know how a person can be a Christian and not have doubts from time to time.* Faith requires doubt in order to be faith. If you ever come to a place where all your doubts are gone and all your questions are answered, take a deep breath and relax because you've arrived in heaven.

Three Kinds of Doubt

Doubt itself is not sinful or wrong. Often it can be the catalyst to new spiritual growth. As I have pondered the matter, I have concluded our doubts tend to fall into three categories: *First, there are intellectual doubts.* These are doubts most often raised by those outside the Christian faith. Is the Bible the Word of God? Is Jesus the Son of God? Did he really rise from the dead? Is Jesus really the only way to heaven?

Second, there are spiritual doubts. These tend to be the doubts of those inside the church. Am I really a Christian? Have I truly believed? Why is it so hard to pray? Why do I still feel guilty? Why is it taking me so long to get better?

Third, there are circumstantial doubts. This is the largest category because it encompasses all the "whys" of life. Why did my child die? Why did my marriage break up? Why can't I find a husband? Why did my friend betray me? Where was God when my uncle was abusing me? These are the questions we meet at the intersection of biblical faith and the pain of living in a fallen world. In my experience, these are the toughest doubts of all. Unfortunately, sometimes we tend to sweep them under the rug and to put down those in the church who struggle with these issues. When we refuse to deal with circumstantial doubts, they soon become spiritual doubts, and those spiritual doubts eventually become intellectual doubts. Then people start leaving the church altogether.

Three Crucial Statements

Lee Strobel frames the issue this way:

1) Many people think doubt is the opposite of faith, but it isn't. Unbelief is the opposite of faith. Unbelief refers to a willful refusal to believe, while doubt refers to inner uncertainty.

2) Many people think doubt is unforgivable, but it isn't. God doesn't condemn us when we question him. Both Job and David repeatedly questioned God, but they were not condemned. God is big enough to handle all our doubts and all our questions.

3) Many people think struggling with God means we lack faith, but that's not true. Very nearly the opposite of that statement is true. Struggling with God is a sure sign that we truly have faith. If we never struggle, our faith will never grow.

Many Christians struggle with doubt and then feel guilty. It is to those believers that my words are directed. In order to get a biblical perspective, let's focus on one godly man who doubted and how Jesus dealt with his doubt.

A Question for Jesus

Do you recall the occasion when Herod threw John the Baptist in jail because John dared to rebuke him for his gross sexual sin? It helps to remember that John went to prison not for doing wrong, but for doing right. He was a mighty preacher of the truth whom God used to prepare the nation for the coming of Christ. Yet here he is, in Herod's prison, in a dungeon, in the wilderness east of the Dead Sea. He didn't know when or if he would be released.

Days passed, then weeks, then months. Prison time is hard time. The days are long, the nights even longer. No doubt confused and frustrated by his incarceration, John sent messengers to Jesus with a very pertinent question: "Are you the one who was to come, or should we expect someone else?" (Matthew 11:2–3). That's a powerful question if you think about it. Having read a few of the commentaries on this passage, I am struck by how many of them feel uneasy with John's doubt. They seem to want to explain it away. On one level, I can understand their discomfort. After all, we know John had made one of the earliest public confessions of Jesus when he cried out, "Look, the Lamb of God, who takes away the sin of the world!" (John 1:29). Then he said, "I have seen and I testify that this is the Son of God" (v. 34). Make no mistake. John knew who Jesus was. How could a man who was so certain about Jesus now harbor such doubt? The text does not provide an exact answer to that question, but I think I know part of the answer.

In 2000 I wrote a short "gospel book" for Moody Publishers called *An Anchor for the Soul*. It's a simple presentation of the gospel in "Walmart English" for people who don't go to church and don't know much about the Bible. Over the last sixteen years we have given away over 800,000 copies, most of them to prisoners through a partnership with Prison Fellowship and Good News Jail and

Prison Ministries. As a result, we have received over 12,000 letters from prisoners. Until I started reading those letters, I knew very little about what it's like to be in prison. My heart has been deeply moved by the accounts of the hopelessness most of them feel. *No place on earth is more corrosive to faith than a prison cell.* No place on earth is darker and more hopeless than a prison cell. I received a letter from a prisoner who said, "Being in prison is like being dead. No one wants anything to do with you." One inmate called prison "Satan's playground."

It is no wonder that as he languished in prison, not knowing when, or if, he would be released, John began to wonder, and then he began to doubt. He at least knew enough to ask the right question. "Are you the one sent from heaven, or is there someone else who will be our Savior? Are you really the promised Messiah?" The answer our Lord gives is very instructive. He does not rebuke John or put him down. He simply gives John the evidence he needs to regain his faith. Go back, he says, and tell John what you have seen. Then he lists six miracles:

The blind see.
The lame walk.
The lepers are cured.
The deaf hear.
The dead are raised.
The poor have the gospel preached to them.

Jesus essentially says, "Go back and tell John that in my name, the hurting people of the world are being totally transformed." This is what people outside the church want to know:

Where is the power that can break the chains of sin?
Where is the power that can save my marriage?
Where is the power that can bring my prodigal son back home?

The people of the world don't understand theology, and most of them don't know much about the Bible. They aren't interested in hearing more theories. But they will listen to anyone who can tell them where to find a fresh start and a new life.

"He's Still My Man"

Notice what happens next:

> As John's disciples were leaving, Jesus began to speak to the crowd about John: "What did you go out into the desert to see? A reed swayed by the wind? If not, what did you go out to see? A man dressed in fine clothes? No, those who wear fine clothes are in kings' palaces. Then what did you go out to see? A prophet? Yes, I tell you, and more than a prophet. This is the one about whom it is written: 'I will send my messenger ahead of you, who will prepare your way before you.' I tell you the truth: Among those born of women there has not risen anyone greater than John the Baptist" (vv. 7-11).

John the Baptist sent his disciples from the prison to find Jesus in Galilee and ask him the all-important question. After giving his answer, Jesus then shares with the crowd his high praise for John the Baptist. He is "more than a prophet," he is the forerunner who was foretold in the Old Testament. No one born of woman has been greater than John the Baptist. Note when Jesus says this. According to verse 7, it happened *as John's disciples were leaving.* That means they heard the high praise of their master and no doubt relayed it to him. But where was John at this point?

He's still in prison.
He's still wrestling with his doubts.
He's still living with uncertainty.

He's still unsure about Jesus.

He hasn't heard the answer yet. It's as if Jesus is saying, "John may doubt me, but I don't doubt him. He's still my man. He's still on my team. I still believe in him." *He affirmed his faith in John while John still had his doubts.* He knew that underneath those doubts there was genuine faith. Jesus is saying, "He's still my man, doubts and all." What an incredible affirmation.

Doubters Welcome!

Above the front door of every church in the world, we should erect a two-word sign: Doubters Welcome! That should be the church's message.

If you have doubts, come inside.
If you have questions, come inside.
If you are uncertain, come inside.
If you are a skeptic, come inside.
If you are searching for truth, come inside.

Deep doubt is often the prelude to an even deeper faith. I love the way Frederick Buechner expresses it: "Doubts are the ants in the pants of faith. They keep it awake and moving" (from the book *Wishful Thinking*). The greatest doubters often become the strongest believers. And honest doubts—once resolved—often become the bedrock of an unshakable faith. It has been said no truth is so strongly believed as that which you once doubted.

Four Ways to Deal with Doubt

Doubt will not disqualify you as a disciple, but it can be dangerous if you don't deal with it. It's what you do with your doubt that matters. Here are four principles to help you handle your doubt:

1: Admit your doubts and ask for help.

That's what the father did in Mark 9:24 when he cried out, "I believe. Help me overcome my unbelief." That's what John the Baptist did. And in a way, that's what Thomas did also. He plainly stated why he could not and would not believe until he saw the evidence for himself. *God is not fragile.* He can handle your doubts, your fears, your worries, and all your unanswered questions. He's a big God. He runs the universe without any help. Your doubts won't upset him. Tell him all your questions and all your doubts, cry out and ask for his help. And don't fight the battle alone. Go to a Christian friend, a pastor, an elder, a deacon, anyone with strong faith and godly insight. Ask them to walk with you as you face your doubts honestly.

2: Act on your faith, not your doubts.

That's what Noah did when he built the ark. That's what Abraham did when he left Ur of the Chaldees. That's what Moses did when he marched through the Red Sea on dry ground. That's what David did when he faced Goliath. That's what Joshua did when he marched around Jericho. That's what Daniel did when he was thrown into the lion's den. That's what Nehemiah did when he built the wall.

Don't you think all these great heroes of the faith had their doubts? Of course they did. They didn't know in advance how everything was going to come out. But they took a deep breath, decided to trust God, and they acted on their faith and not on their doubts. If you do the same thing, your faith will continually grow stronger.

3: Doubt your doubts, not your faith.

This simply means you should not cast away your faith because you are in the deep valley of darkness. All of us walk into that valley from time to time. Some of us spend a great deal of time there. When you find yourself in that valley where all is uncertain and you are sorely tempted to give in to your doubts, fears and worries, remember these two words: keep walking. You may be in a valley of doubt today, but you don't have to stop and build a condo there. The only way out is to keep on walking. Every step forward is a way to "doubt your doubts." Soon enough the light will shine again.

#4: Keep going back to what you know to be true.

This is the crucial point. After considering the sufferings of this life, and the perils and tribulations of following Christ, Paul concludes Romans 8 triumphantly by declaring that nothing in all the universe can separate us from the love of God in Christ Jesus our Lord. In 2 Timothy 1:12 he says, "I know whom I have believed."

Some things you think.
Some things you hope.
Some things you feel.
Some things you know.

Faith is not a feeling. Sometimes we talk about "feeling God's presence" during a worship service. I know what people mean when they talk like that. I'm all for having a consciousness of God's presence in your life. But what will you do when the happy feeling goes away? If all you have is a "God of the good times," you don't have the God of the Bible. What will you do when the boss says, "We're letting you go" What will you do when your spouse walks out of your marriage? What will you do when the doctor says, "I'm sorry. There's nothing else we can do"? What will you do when your children end up in jail? We need a faith big enough to encompass the worst moments of life.

Going "All In"

When I was younger, I thought I had everything figured out. Life has a way of knocking us down a few pegs. That certainly happened to me. I'm not as sure about some of the details as I was 30 years ago. *But what I know, I really know.* I have a handful of convictions that cannot be shaken. I would include in that short list these truths: God is good, Jesus is Lord, the Bible is true, this world is not my home, and even hard times are meant for my benefit. At the core of my faith is an unshakable belief in the sovereignty of God. He's God and I'm not. He is sovereign over all the details of my life, and I can trust him completely even when those details seem to be spinning out of control.

Years ago I decided to go "all in" on Jesus. I'm "all in" that he is the Son of God, that he died on the cross for my sins, that he rose from the dead on the third day, that he is the Lord of the universe, that he is coming again, and that he will someday take me to heaven. Lewis Sperry Chafer said believing in Jesus means trusting him so much that if he can't take you to heaven, you aren't going to go there. I like that. If Jesus can't take me to heaven, then I'll never make it because I'm going "all in" on him. I don't have a plan B.

I ran across a statement that resonated with my own heart: "One who has never doubted has only half believed." By that standard, I'm not ashamed to say I have fully believed because I have often doubted. But my doubts have only made my faith stronger in the end.

Just As I Am

In the 1830s a young woman named Charlotte Elliott was visiting some friends in the West End of London when she met a noted minister named Cesar Malan. Over supper he asked if she was a Christian. When she replied she did not want to talk about the subject, the minister said, "I did not mean to offend you. But I want you to know Jesus can save you if you will turn to him." When they met again several weeks later, Miss Elliott said she had been trying to come to Christ but did not know how to do it. "Just come to him as you are," Mr. Malan said. Taking the advice to heart, she composed a poem that began this way:

> Just as I am, without one plea
> but that thy blood was shed for me,

And that thou bidd'st me come to thee,
O Lamb of God, I come, I come!

The third verse contains Charlotte Elliott's own testimony:

Just as I am, though tossed about,
with many a conflict, many a doubt.
Fightings and fears within, without,
O Lamb of God, I come, I come!

And the last verse contains the gospel promise:

Just as I am, thou wilt receive,
wilt welcome, pardon, cleanse, relieve;
Because thy promise I believe,
O Lamb of God, I come, I come!

My doubting brothers and sisters, take heart.

Do not despair.
Don't let your doubts take you away from Jesus.
Let your doubts lead you to Jesus.
Keep believing.

Come to him with your doubts, your skepticism, your unbelief, your hard questions, your uncertainties. Don't let your doubts keep you from Jesus. Come to him just as you are—and bring your doubts with you.

Take your fears to Jesus.
Take your questions to Jesus.
Take your doubts to Jesus.

He never turns an honest doubter away.

Here is a very simple prayer that could help you believe all over again. I encourage you to say this prayer out loud and then write it down or print it out where you can see it every day.

Lord God, take your Word and seal it to my heart. I believe you are who you said you are, and I believe you will do what you said you will do. Fill me with your Holy Spirit so I might move from doubt to faith. Thank you for not turning away when I am weak, fearful, and confused. Help me to go all in on Jesus with nothing held back. Amen.

10

WHY IS LIFE SO HARD?

The call came at about 10:30 P.M. Someone had died. Would I please call the family? Before I could pick up the phone, the mother called me. Her son had taken drugs and had died earlier that evening. As I got dressed to go to the home, I wondered what I would say. When I got there everyone was milling around in a state of confusion. At length, the mother took me aside and through her tears, asked me the inevitable question, the question I had known was coming. Why? Why did God let this happen to my son?

It was not the first time I have had no satisfactory answer to that question, and it won't be the last. For when you look at the questions of life and death, and when you consider the problems of this death-sentenced generation, even the most fervent believer looks up to the heavens and cries out, "Why? Why me? Why now? Why this?"

Why? The question rings across the centuries and through every generation. All of us ask it sooner or later. If you haven't yet, you will. *It's a question that does not admit of an easy answer.* Indeed, the godliest believers have sometimes wondered about the ways of God. And if Job never got a complete answer, what can I expect? As I read the Bible, I don't think there is one single answer to that question.

An Unexpected Answer

But there are answers. And men and women of faith have found them true throughout the centuries. One answer tucked away in the Bible may surprise you. It is found in a New Testament book we don't read very much: Second Corinthians. In the first verses of the first chapter, we discover a perspective on the heartaches of life that may help us. After a brief greeting to his readers (vv. 1-2) in which Paul (along with Timothy) wishes grace and peace to his readers in Corinth and throughout the surrounding region, he immediately begins to talk about the comfort he had received in the midst of much hardship he had endured as an apostle of Jesus Christ. *Verses 3–11 set the stage for the whole book by plainly saying that no matter what he had suffered, it was more than worth it.*

Here we learn right up front an essential principle for all of life. *It's not what happens to us that matters; it's how we react that makes all the difference.* Years ago a friend told me, "When hard times come, be a student, not a victim." Think about that for a moment.

A victim says, "Why did this happen to me?"
A student says, "What can I learn from this?"

A victim believes his hard times have come because God is trying to punish him.
A student understands that God allows hard times to help him grow.

A victim believes God has abandoned him.
A student sees God's hand in everything, including the worst moments of life.

That's the true Christian position. We believe so much in the sovereignty of God that when hard times come, we believe—no, we know!—that God is at work somehow, somewhere, in some way for our good and his glory. Paul says as much in Romans 8:28. As he begins this letter to the Corinthians, he spells out the same truth in a slightly different way. *Here we discover how affliction works four positive benefits for us.*

1: It draws us closer to the Lord.

"Praise be to the God and Father of our Lord Jesus Christ, the Father of compassion and the God of all comfort, who comforts us in all our troubles, so that we can comfort those in any trouble with the comfort we ourselves have received from God. For just as the sufferings of Christ flow over into our lives, so also through Christ our comfort overflows." (vv. 3-5).

There is a divine purpose at work in your life and in mine, and that divine purpose begins with God. Paul calls him the "Father of compassion." I learned about this many years ago. When our oldest son was still an infant, he often didn't want to go to bed at night. We would put him in his crib, and then Marlene would go to bed exhausted from the cares of the day. About 30 minutes later Joshua would begin to cry. I would roll over in bed and put the pillow over my head, hoping that the noise would go away. Eventually I would go to Joshua's room and pick him up. Holding him with his head on my shoulder, I would walk around the house singing to him. Sometimes I would sing familiar songs, and sometimes it would be "Good little boys don't cry, cry, cry." We would walk back and forth through the night. I wasn't a good singer by any means, but my singing seemed to help settle him down. After 30 minutes, Joshua would finally fall asleep. I would put him back to bed and go back to bed myself. Now I'm not a perfect father, but I would do that for my son. Would God do any less for me? No, he would do far more. He is a Father of Compassion.

Notice what verse 4 says: "Who comforts us in *all* our troubles." That means that when I am sick, he is there by my bedside. When I run out of money, he is there with me in my poverty. When I am hated and despised, he stands by my side. And when I walk through the valley of the shadow of death, he takes me by the hand, and he leads me on through.

We never discover the depth of God's compassion until we get in a place where we need God's compassion desperately. You don't receive mercy until you are in real trouble. During a dinner conversation with another couple, the husband mentioned that he had been diagnosed with a very serious form of cancer. As sometimes happens, cancer came despite the fact that he kept himself in very good physical condition. It started with a pain that seemed like a pulled muscle. When the doctor made the cancer diagnosis, my friend was told that he was almost at Stage 4. After a harrowing round of chemotherapy, he seems to be in remission. But it's the sort of cancer that often comes back so you never feel totally at ease. When I asked how the cancer had impacted him spiritually, he said that now he feels more relaxed. Things that used to bother him don't bother him as much. Cancer, it seems, has clarified the priorities of his life. He also remarked that he has become a much stronger believer in the sovereignty of God, that God is in control of all things, right down to the tiniest details of life. He concluded by saying, "I've come to see that sickness can sometimes be a blessing."

The Apostle Paul would no doubt agree. *Cancer is not easy or fun, and it is not "good" in and of itself.* But cancer can be the channel for much good if in your sickness, you discover what matters and what doesn't. And it will be a very deep blessing if through your sickness, you discover that God's comfort is greater than your sorrow.

And that comfort leads on to the second benefit from our affliction…

#2: It equips us to minister to others.

"If we are distressed, it is for your comfort and salvation; if we are comforted, it is for your comfort, which produces in you patient endurance of the same sufferings we suffer. And our hope for you is firm, because we know that just as you share in our sufferings, so also you share in our comfort" (vv. 6-7).

Paul looked at his sufferings—the hardship, deprivation, imprisonment, the unrelenting opposition he faced, and he concluded, "This isn't just for me. God is doing something in me for the benefit of others."

We never suffer alone.

Someone else is always watching. Our friends watch to see how we will respond to tragedy. They want to know if what we say we believe is really enough for us in the hard times. And further in the distance, others watch what we go through. Many of them are unbelievers who wonder if Christ is real. They don't know, they aren't sure, maybe they've read the Bible, maybe they haven't, but they're watching how we respond to mistreatment, malicious accusations, sickness, the loss of a job, the end of our marriage, a career setback, a financial collapse, and from the shadows they peer out to watch the suffering saint to see if what he has is real or not.

That's exactly what Paul is talking about. *Our afflictions soften our hearts so that when we have received the comfort of God, it is easy for us to pass it along to someone else.* Oh, how we need this in the church of Jesus Christ. It is so easy to be callous. It is so convenient to be unkind. It is so easy to look down our noses at weaker brothers and sisters who go through hard times. We say so carelessly, "Why don't they just get tough? Why don't they show some backbone? Why don't they quit complaining and get on with life? Why can't they be strong like the rest of us?" God lets us go through hard times to break us of that attitude and soften us up so that we are able to minister in the name of Jesus Christ to other hurting people.

Chuck Colson went to prison and out of that harrowing experience he founded Prison Fellowship. Joni Erickson Tada was paralyzed during a diving accident and out of her suffering came a worldwide ministry to the hurting called Joni and Friends. This should not surprise us because the Lord's strongest weapons are forged on the anvil of adversity.

This mighty principle answers many questions. *Many of us have hardened places in our lives that will not become tender until we go through the fires of affliction.* God lets that happen so that we might reach out to others and comfort them.

Our affliction produces a third benefit ...

#3: It empties us of all self-reliance.

"We do not want you to be uninformed, brothers, about the hardships we suffered in the province of Asia. We were under great pressure, far beyond our ability to endure, so that we despaired even of life. Indeed, in our hearts we felt the sentence of death. But this happened that we might not rely on ourselves but on God, who raises the dead. He has delivered us from such a deadly peril, and he will deliver us. On him we have set our hope that he will continue to deliver us" (vv. 8-10).

We don't know the exact nature of the hardships Paul suffered in Asia (modern-day Turkey). It might have been extreme opposition from the Jewish leaders. It might have been some sort of serious physical ailment. Whatever it was, the Corinthians knew about it, and they understood that Paul thought during his ordeal that he was going to die. He writes to tell of God's deliverance and to ask the Corinthians for their prayers.

When tragedy strikes or when hard times come or when friends turn against us or when the bottom drops out of life, we wonder why things happen the way they do. Here we find one important explanation. *Hard times come to teach us not to trust in ourselves but only in the Lord who raises the dead.* Most of us are adept at handling the "moderate" problems of life. We can deal with cranky children or a prickly boss or a bad case of the flu or a pile of work that gets dumped on our desk. We understand normal pressures, and we learn how to deal with them. But sometimes things happen that "strip the gears" of life and force us to our knees and sometimes all the way down so that we are flat on the ground. At that point, when all human options are foreclosed, our only hope is the Lord. We cry out to God in desperation, knowing that if he doesn't help us, we're sunk. That's a lesson we have to learn over and over again.

There is one final thing that affliction does for us …

#4: It reveals the power of prayer.

"As you help us by your prayers. Then many will give thanks on our behalf for the gracious favor granted us in answer to the prayers of many" (v. 11).

I love that phrase, "you help us by your prayers." Paul uses a Greek word that occurs only here in the New Testament. It's a compound word that comes from three other words meaning "with," "under," and "work." It's what the Amish do when they have a barn raising. They literally get under the frame, lifting it up together, and holding it up so that it can put in the right place. In the same way we join together and lift the burdens of life as we pray for each other.

Many times we view prayer as the last resort when it ought to be the first resort. I know that prayer sometimes seems futile because we think we need to "do something." Praying is fine, but how about if we bake a cake? Well, that's fine too. But don't fall into the trap of separating life into the "spiritual" and the "practical," as if baking a cake is "real help" while prayer is just something spiritual we do when we can't do anything else. Very nearly the opposite is true. *Through prayer we unleash the power of heaven for the problems we face on the earth.* So we ought to pray more, not less in times of trouble.

An email arrived from a friend whose child has suddenly been diagnosed with an extremely rare form of cancer that seemed to come out of nowhere.

> Two weeks ago, we thought she had a hernia. This has all been very unreal and we are leaning heavily on God and all the people he has placed around us to support us as we walk this road.

Knowing that others are praying for us gives us strength to keep going. *God has ordained that our prayers matter.* Pause over that thought for a moment.

Our prayers matter.

It makes a difference whether or not we pray. Paul is saying, "When I thought I was going to die, you prayed and God delivered me." *We will never know until we get to heaven how many times the prayers of others rescued us.* But I believe in that great day, when all the secrets are revealed, we will discover that we would have fallen, but someone prayed for us.

We would have given up, but someone prayed for us.
We would have made a stupid decision, but someone prayed for us.
We would have given in to temptation, but someone prayed for us.
We would have retaliated, but someone prayed for us.
We would have crumbled under pressure, but someone prayed for us.

When all is said and done, we will learn that God used the prayers of others to enable us to make the journey from earth to heaven, and we will discover that without those God-inspired prayers, we never would have made it.

I have a friend who pastors in China where there is much opposition to the gospel. He has recently received some pressure from various officials about his ministry. When I wrote to tell him that many people were praying for him, he wrote back an email to say thanks. I will simply replicate the first and last sentences of that email (including the all-caps of the last sentence):

> I am so honored to receive your 2 emails about loving and caring for me and my situation! Surely that touched my heart and my spirit greatly!
>
> IN HIS LOVE THANK YOU ALL WHO ARE PRAYING FOR ME, AND YOU SHOULD KNOW THAT IS THE MOST IMPORTANT HELP TO ME IN THIS SITUATION!

He is living out the truth of this passage.

Pebbles in the Water

We ought to pray for others, and we ought to give thanks together when our prayers are answered. When we pray, we join hands with God to bless others and to advance his cause on the earth. Through united prayer we knock holes in the darkness to let the light of Jesus shine in. This is why "the devil trembles when he sees, the weakest saint upon his knees."

No one is exempt from the trials of life. Becoming a Christian is wonderful, but it does not free you from the burdens of life. *In many ways becoming a Christian may increase your troubles because of spiritual opposition you face.* When hard times come, we only have two choices:

We can suffer with God, or
We can suffer without God.

That much I have said many times. But now I want to add something to that. When hard times come …

We can suffer by ourselves, or
We can suffer with the people of God.

As we receive comfort, we are equipped to minister to others. We then pass along to others what God has given to us. *This is the very essence of Christianity.*

From God
To us
To others.

Have you ever gone to a pond out in the country and thrown a pebble into the water? What happens? From the point where the pebble enters the water, ripples spread out farther and farther. What starts as a ripple from one small pebble soon affects the whole pond. That's a picture of what God is doing in your life. *He comforts you in your trials so that you might comfort another who may comfort another who may comfort another.* And the ripple effect spreads out from you to people you may never even meet.

Some believers never discover this truth. They are perpetual gripers when things get difficult. Life is never fair, they always get the short end of the stick, God has singled them out for punishment. Such people never have a ministry to others because they constantly fight against God's perspective on their trials and remain tough and hardened when they ought to be soft and tender. As a result, they have nothing to pass along to anyone else.

Missionary Eyes

May I suggest one simple step of application? Many of us would like a personal ministry, but we don't know where to begin. This passage suggests that our personal ministry begins as we share with others what God has shared with us. *That means there are people in your life who need the help only you can give.* Some of them need a word of encouragement, and you are the only one who can give them that word. Some of them are staggering beneath a heavy load, and you are the only one who can lift that burden from their shoulders. Some of them are about to quit, and you are the only one who can keep them in the race. Some of them have been hit with an incredible string of trials, and you are the only one who can help them keep going.

Those people are all around you. Your only problem is that you don't see them. *Pray that God will give you Missionary Eyes.* Those are eyes that see the real needs of the people you meet. Pray that God will bring at least one person across your path who needs the help only you can give. That's a prayer God will answer since there are folks all around you who are just barely making it. You see them where you work, and you live next door to them. Your children go to school with their children. They are out there waiting for someone to give them help. And we have experienced the goodness of the Lord.

God has helped us so that we might take what we have received and share it with those who desperately need it.

You may have heard the term "wounded healer." We are all wounded with the failures of life and the burdens that weigh us down. God has committed to wounded men and women the great ministry of sharing his love with others.

Don't waste your pain. Use it to grow closer to the Lord and to his people. Use it as a means to minister to others. May God raise up an army of "wounded healers" who will take the comfort they have received and in Jesus' name offer it to a hurting, waiting, watching world.

11

PRAYING FOR YOUR PRODIGAL

I received an email with a heartrending question:

> I have a daughter that I don't believe is saved. I pray
> for her but often times I can't. I suppose I'm angry
> she isn't responding and feel incapable of helping
> her. What can I pray for on a daily basis so she will
> come to Christ? At times I feel such sorrow, thinking
> she might go to hell.

This parent speaks for mothers and fathers everywhere who pray
for their prodigal children, often for years, with seemingly no results.
I do not doubt that praying parents must at some point feel like
giving up, and it must be hard not to get angry when you see your
children repeatedly making bad choices or showing no interest in
the gospel. What do you do then? How do you keep believing for
your own prodigal son or daughter?

When I use the word "prodigal," I'm referring to anyone who has
drifted away from their Christian heritage. It could refer to a college
student who simply stops going to church or to a man who thinks

he doesn't need "religion" or to someone who becomes an atheist. It could refer to a son raised in the church who calmly tells his mother, "I'm no longer a Christian." A prodigal could be a husband who one day walks out on his marriage and simply disappears. A prodigal could be someone who gets so busy in their career that they have no time for God.

In thinking about cases like this, we often wonder if the prodigal is saved or lost. *The answer is, only God knows because only he can read the heart.* We don't need to answer the "Are they saved?" question because for the moment we don't know the answer. It's usually not profitable to spend time wondering, "Were they ever truly converted?" Those questions, while important, go to matters of the heart known only to the Lord.

When we look from the outside, it may be easy to conclude that the person we thought we knew so well was never saved in the first place. But our knowledge is limited. While the prodigal may appear to have totally rejected his background, and he may give all the appearances of being lost, only God knows for certain.

The Problem We Face

When thinking about hard questions, it's crucial that we start in the right place. Nowhere is this more important than when we pray for our prodigal sons and daughters. Because we have so much invested in them, we may be tempted to give up because the pain of praying when nothing seems to be happening finally overwhelms us.

A prodigal may be a pastor who ran off with a woman in his church and now has rejected his family and his faith. It might refer to a brother who used to be an Awana leader who now refuses to go to church at all. It could refer to a Bible college graduate who now lives an openly homosexual lifestyle. You may have learned about Jesus from someone who now rejects the very faith they once taught you. Very often prodigals start out as people who, having been deeply hurt by the circumstances of life, feel abandoned or cheated or mistreated by God.

These things happen, and they happen more often than we like to admit. If we could go behind the scenes of the "best" Christian families we know, most of them would have stories of a prodigal son or daughter or a prodigal husband or wife. There is no way to guarantee it won't happen to someone close to you. For that matter, I know of no way to be certain that you may not become a prodigal someday. That's why we have warnings in the New Testament to pay attention to how we live and to take nothing for granted (1 Corinthians 9:24–27 is a good example).

In stating the matter this way, I don't believe I am a pessimist. I am drawing conclusions based on a sober reading of the New Testament and a lifetime of dealing with hurting, confused people.

The parable Jesus told that gave us the term "prodigal son" (Luke 15:11–32) is universally regarded as one of the greatest short stories ever told because it speaks truth about the human condition.

Prodigals happen.
This is the problem we face.

They won't come back until they are ready.
We can't argue them back or shame them back.
If we force them back too early, they will still be in the "far country" on the inside.

How should we pray for our prodigals? To answer that, we first need to get our theology right.

The Theology We Need

We need to remember that an astounding miracle lies at the heart of our faith. We believe something incredible—that a man who was dead came back to life on the third day. We believe God raised him from the dead. Now if God would do that for his Son, indeed if God has the power to raise the dead, who are we to question God's power to change the hardest hearts? After all, if you go to the cemetery and stay there waiting for a resurrection, you'll wait a long time. You will see plenty of funerals but no resurrections. What are the chances that a man who had been tortured and then crucified and then buried in a tomb would be raised from the dead? *The odds would seem to be against it.* You can't start with what your eyes see or what you can figure out. You can't trust your feelings because your emotions can play tricks on you. We must therefore start with God who can raise the dead, not with the person who is spiritually dead.

If it is God alone who can raise the dead, then our focus must be on God alone.

Here are three verses that will help us as we think about praying for our prodigals:

> "Above all else, guard your heart, for everything you do flows from it" (Proverbs 4:23 NIV).

> "The king's heart is a stream of water in the hand of the Lord; he turns it wherever he will" (Proverbs 21:1 ESV).

> "I pray that the eyes of your heart may be enlightened" (Ephesians 1:18 NASB).

The heart has eyes. Did you know that? When Paul speaks of "your heart," he's not referring to the organ in your chest that pumps blood throughout your body. The term "heart" refers to what we might call "the real you," the place inside where the decisions of life are made. The heart decides what values you will live by and what direction you will go and how you will live your life each day. *Every important decision you make starts in your heart.*

Your heart has eyes that can be open or closed. When the eyes of your heart are closed to the light of God, you stumble blindly through life, making one dumb choice after another. You fall into sinful patterns, you break God's laws, you make the same mistakes over and over again, and you enter one dead-end relationship after another. Why? Because the eyes of your heart are shut and you lack moral vision. The light of God is shut out of your life. *That means you can see and be blind at the same time.* There are lots of people like that in the world. Physically they can see, but spiritually they are blind.

That describes many young people raised in the church. *They know God, but their eyes are so filled with the things of the world that they are blind to the truth.* Let me illustrate. Here we have a young man who has been raised in a Christian home. He's been going to church for years—Sunday School, Vacation Bible School, children's ministry, and the youth group. Now he goes off to college where he's on his own. He meets a girl, and they start dating. Soon they are sleeping together. When his parents hear about it, they are furious and worried and upset, and they wonder what to do. They argue and plead and cajole and threaten and quote Scripture, all to no avail. What is the problem? It is precisely this: *The eyes of his heart are closed to the truth of God.* Until those eyes are opened, all the yelling in the world won't make much difference.

If our young people sleep around, or if they get drunk on the weekends, if they cheat and cut corners, if they are rebellious and unmotivated, those things are only symptoms of a deeper, more fundamental issue. *They've never made a personal commitment to get serious about Jesus Christ.* Once Christ becomes the center of your life, no one will have to tell you not to sleep around, and no one will have to tell you, "Don't get drunk on the weekends." You just won't do it. Once the eyes of your heart are opened, the light of God's truth will come flooding in, and you'll never look at anything the same way again.

The Prayer We Must Pray

The heart of the problem is the problem of the heart.

Sometimes we worry too much about the symptoms without dealing with the root issues of life. We should pray, "Open the eyes of their heart, Lord," because when that happens, life will radically change. They will grab their helmet and get in the ballgame for the Lord. They'll go to the huddle and say, "You call the play, Lord. I'm ready to do whatever you say."

One translation of Ephesians 1:18 (The Voice) says it this way: "Open the eyes of their hearts, and let the light of Your truth flood in."

That's what prodigals need.
That's what we all need.

It's a beautiful picture of a person whose eyes have been closed for a long time. When their eyes are opened, light from heaven comes flooding in.

Suddenly everything looks different.
What seemed right, they now see as wrong.
The truth they once mocked, they now gladly obey.
The Jesus they spurned, they now worship.
The path they followed into sin, they follow no more.

All things have become new to them.
What a thousand sermons could not do, the light of God does for them.

Once they enjoyed the far country.
Now they long to dwell in the Father's house.

Once they lived for worldly pleasure.
Now they seek to please the Lord.

Once sin held them captive.
Now their heart is captive to Jesus alone.

Some people wonder, "Is this possible?" Could a life so far gone in sin ever be deeply changed? My answer is quite simple: *We do not need to understand how it could happen.* We only need to know that with God all things are possible.

Opening blind eyes is the supernatural work of the Holy Spirit. He alone can do it, but he *can* do it, and this is the source of our hope.

This is why we pray for our children and grandchildren and our family members and for friends and loved ones who today are far from God. As we think about our prodigals, we should cry out to God and say, "O Lord, open the eyes of their heart. Help them to see the light of truth." That prayer is so simple and yet so profound. *Only God can open the eyes of the heart.* When God opens those eyes, they will see the truth and light from heaven will come flooding in.

A Mother's Tears

My favorite story about the power of prayer to reclaim a prodigal is over 1,600 years old. It begins with a woman named Monica, who was raised by Christian parents in North Africa. When she was old enough, her parents arranged a marriage to a pagan man. Evidently the marriage was very difficult because of divided spiritual loyalties. Monica and her husband had three children who survived. *Two of them followed Christ, but one son left the faith of his childhood.* By his own admission, he chose the path of worldly pleasure. For many years he lived with a mistress and together they gave birth to a son out of wedlock. He broke his mother's heart by joining a religious cult. Monica prayed for 17 years that her son would return to Christ.

Looking back, her son said she watered the earth with her tears for him, praying more for his spiritual death than most mothers pray over the physical death of a child. She fasted and prayed and asked God to save her son. One day she went to see the bishop and with tears asked why her son was still living in sin. The bishop replied with words that have become famous across the centuries: "It is not possible that the son of so many tears should perish. Your son will be saved." He was right. *It took several more years of fervent praying, but eventually Monica's son came to Christ.* His name is Augustine. We know him today as Saint Augustine. He is universally regarded as one of the greatest thinkers in Christian history. He makes it clear that his mother prayed him to Jesus. She would not give up, and eventually God answered her prayers.

I think the bishop was right when he said, "It is not possible that the son of so many tears should perish." How precious are a mother's tears! There are mothers and grandmothers who have prayed their children and their grandchildren to Christ. They have seen their children and grandchildren in the "far country" of sin and have prayed them step by step back to the Father's House. When everyone else gave up, godly women laid hold of heaven and claimed their offspring in Jesus' name.

Please do not misunderstand. I do not believe our prayers contain merit in and of themselves. *But God has ordained both the means and the ends of salvation.* We pray because everything depends on God, and we preach because the gospel is the power of God for salvation. *Your prayers are part of heaven's plan to reach out to the prodigals in your life and bring them back to God.* If you are heavily burdened for a loved one, you may be sure that the burden does not come from yourself. The burden is a gift from God, a token of his mercy toward the prodigal who at this moment cares nothing for the Lord. Your prayers are an indispensable link in the chain of God's purposes.

First, We Must Change

I received an email with a perspective we need to consider:

> Our third son is a prodigal (although I suppose we are ALL prodigals in some fashion!). I have experienced a depth of relationship with God that I didn't know before mothering a prodigal. God has continued to walk this road of parenting with us, revealing his character to us, and growing us through the trials. I thank God for our son because he has been the iron that sharpens me. I trust God is working deep in his heart, even though the outside doesn't often look that way. I believe someday his eyes will be

opened, and God will remove his heart of stone and will give him a heart of flesh! And the renewing of his heart and his mind will be a great testimony to God and who he is.

Everything I have been trying to say is in that email. Here is a mother who has grown spiritually as she has prayed for her son. Instead of becoming bitter, she has been changed on the inside and brought closer to the Lord. *God often uses the prodigals in our lives to bring us closer to him.* As long as we try to control our loved ones, either through anger or through our tears or by arguing with them or complaining about them to others, as long as we focus on them, they will not change, and neither will we. Sometimes in our despair, we become prodigals ourselves because our anger at them has ruined our own walk with the Lord.

As we pray for our prodigals, remember that the change we seek must start with us. Until we are changed, and our anger is turned to love, we will become bitter and hardened ourselves. That can happen even though we go to church every Sunday, pray the prayers, sing the songs, serve the Lord, and do all the outward things the church asks us to do. At that point we have become prodigals just as surely as the loved one for whom we are praying.

We must relinquish our loved ones into God's hands and say, "Lord, they belong to you. Always have, always will." *They never were ours to start with.* It is so hard to yield them to the Lord, but we can do it if we remember that his love never fails, that he knows what he is doing, and that he is a better parent than we are.

We sometimes look at the prodigals around us and wonder where God is in the midst of our pain.

He is not unknowing or uncaring.
He is not surprised or stumped.

Though our prodigals may have left the Lord, he has not left them, not even for a second. They may be "lost" to you, but they are not "lost" to him. He knows exactly where they are and what they are doing at this very moment. He loves them more than you do. He leads them even when they don't know they are being led.

Do you have a loved one who is far from the Lord?
Does it seem impossible that he or she will ever change?
Do you get angry thinking about their foolish choices?
Do your prayers seem useless to you?

Pay no attention to your feelings. There is more going on in the heart of your loved one than you can know.

Don't give up.
Keep on praying.
Keep believing.
You never know what God will do.

When you pray for a loved one who seems hardened against the Lord, pray that the eyes of their heart might be opened so the light of God can come flooding in. *If that seems hopeless, at least it puts the hopeless case at God's doorstep, which is where it belongs.* On Saturday night there was a "hopeless case" in the Garden Tomb. On Sunday morning the whole world changed when Jesus rose from the dead. You never know what God will do, so keep on believing and keep on praying. God specializes in impossible situations, and he loves to prove that hopeless cases aren't hopeless after all.

Never give up. Pray, pray, and keep on praying. Your prayers accomplish more than you have ever dreamed.

12

DEATH IS NOT THE END OF OUR STORY

O f all the fears that plague the heart of man, none is greater than the fear of death. It is our greatest fear, the sum of all other fears.

We are afraid to die.

We are afraid of what happens when we die.

Death is the fundamental human problem.

Several years ago a friend sent me an email containing these lines from a poem called "Gray's Elegy" written in a country churchyard in England:

> The boast of heraldry, the pomp of power
> And all that beauty, all that wealth e'er gave
> Awaits alike the inevitable hour
> The paths of glory lead but to the grave.

Life is short and so uncertain. "What is your life? You are a mist that appears for a little while and then vanishes" (James 4:14b). Moses said to the Lord in Psalm 90:5-6, "You sweep men away in the sleep of death; they are like the new grass of the morning-though in the morning it springs up new, by evening it is dry and withered." It is sometimes said nothing is certain in life except death and taxes. But that is not true. A clever man with a good lawyer can find a way around most if not all of his taxes, but no one escapes death.

Worldwide, there are approximately 56,600,000 deaths each year. That works out to 4.7 million per month, 155,000 per day, 6,500 per hour, 107 per minute, and 1.8 per second. The Greek playwright Sophocles said it this way: "Of all the great wonders, none is greater than man. Only for death can he find no cure."

Does death win in the end? *On this side of the grave, it's hard to tell.* Left to our observations, we don't know much beyond the familiar words of Ecclesiastes. There is "a time to be born and a time to die" (Ecclesiastes 3:2). Visit any cemetery, and you can't tell much difference between the Christian and the non-Christian. You can intuit something by reading the markers, but the dead lie buried side by side, six feet underground. There they are, all grouped together, young and old, male and female, rich and poor, famous and infamous, churchgoers and nonbelievers.

Or so it seems.

Death is not the end of the story for those who know the Lord. The Bible tells us what lies ahead for those who know Jesus. In 2 Corinthians 5 we discover truth that gives us hope as we face death with all its dark fears.

This passage is one of the most difficult among all the things Paul wrote, and yet once you get past the difficulties, there is a simplicity about it that attracts the believing heart. Even if we do not understand every detail, the first impression it leaves with the reader gives hope as we look ahead to the end of our earthly journey and wonder, "What's next?" Paul tells us that we have nothing to fear, that no matter how we die or when or where, and no matter what may be our physical condition at the moment of death, we have a promise from God that death itself cannot break.

The Certainty of the Resurrection Body

"Now we know that if the earthly tent we live in is destroyed, we have a building from God, an eternal house in heaven, not built by human hands" (verse 1).

Surely the most important part of this verse comes in the first three words: "Now we know." Death itself confronts us with many mysteries. No one who reads these words can say with certainty how much longer they will live. Not long ago I celebrated my 66th birthday. That means I'm eligible for Social Security, and I'm enrolled in Medicare (that's a sentence I never thought I'd write). Will I live to celebrate my 67th? The odds are in my favor, but the odds are nothing more than actuarial calculations. *Every single breath we take is a gift from God.* I've been breathing for 66 years and not thinking much about it, but it's true. Every single breath is a gift from the Almighty. I am not guaranteed another day, much less another year.

As to what happens after we die, science has nothing useful to tell us. The great researchers have no knowledge about what happens a minute after we die. We will not get the answer from philosophy or from history. If you visit a cemetery, all you know for certain is that it is full of dead people who once were alive. Try as you might, you cannot divine from studying the dead what happens when we die.

There is speculation, and then there is revelation. Paul says there are some things we can know with certainty.

Truth # 1: We live in a tent.

I am not much of a tent man myself. I spent my last night in a tent almost 30 years ago when our oldest son was 2 or 3 years old. On a visit to Yosemite National Park in California, we pitched our tent and went inside for the night. But Josh did not want to go to sleep. He fussed and cried and made so much noise that nearby campers shined their lights in our direction. We ended up vacating the tent and spending the night cramped in our Ford Pinto. That was the end of my camping career.

Our bodies are like tents. They wear out, they sag, they expand, they wrinkle, the joints get creaky, the arteries harden, gravity pulls everything downward, the eyes grow dim, the teeth fall out, the back is stooped, and the arms grow weary. Our bones break, our muscles weaken. The body bulges in the wrong places. We brag about our strength, but a tiny microbe can kill us. Sooner or later we grow old, and our bodies begin to break down. Eventually they stop working altogether. No amount of Vitamin C or Siberian Ginseng can change that fact. At best, we can only slow down the aging process; we cannot delay it forever.

As we age, we pay more attention to things like diet and exercise. Fitness is in. We've got Weight Watchers and Jenny Craig and Curves, and we've got runners and bikers and marathoners and people who lift weights four times a week. We have Plexus and Arbonne. You can work out on a Peloton, or you can do the "Insanity" workout. You can go to LA Fitness or Gold's Gym or to one of those 24-hour gyms where you can exercise at 3 AM if you want to.

All of that is good. Exercise helps and good nutrition is even better, and it would help all of us to get in shape and stay in shape. But I have a bit of news for you. *Your body won't last forever.* You can eat all the low-carb ice cream you want, but your body will still fall apart in the end. Did you know your body disintegrates all the time? *The cells of your body are programmed to die.* The scientific term for this is apoptosis. Each day the average adult loses 50–70 billion cells. That's not a misprint. Before the sun goes down today, between 50 and 70 billion of your cells will die. That's 350 billion cells a week. No wonder you need to lie down and take a nap. You're falling apart even while you read this chapter.

Truth # 2: We will one day trade in our tent for a building.

Think about the difference between a tent and a building. Tents are temporary and flimsy, easily torn, and meant to be replaced. A building is strong, anchored to a foundation, and not meant to be moved.

Someday we will give up our tent and replace it with a building made by God himself. That one fact tells us something important about death.

Death is not the end.
Death is not reincarnation.
Death is not evaporation.
Death is not annihilation.

Death is a trade-in.

One day we will trade in our broken-down bodies for a new body. Look what Paul says about that new body:

It is from God.
It is not made with hands.
It is eternal.
It is heavenly, not earthly.

That's what Paul means when he says, "We know." There are many things we don't know about the future, but this much is certain. *We won't have to live in tents forever.* Someday our "tent" will be replaced with a "building" made by God.

The Nature of the Resurrection Body

"Meanwhile we groan, longing to be clothed with our heavenly dwelling, because when we are clothed, we will not be found naked. For while we are in this tent, we groan and are burdened, because we do not wish to be unclothed but to be clothed with our heavenly dwelling, so that what is mortal may be swallowed up by life" (vv. 2–4).

What will the coming day of resurrection be like? We can find three answers in these verses.

Answer # 1: It is like putting on an overcoat.

When Paul says we long to be clothed, he uses an unusual Greek verb that means something like "to be clothed upon." It has the idea of putting on an overcoat, which is literally a coat put over (or upon) the body. Paul looks forward to the day when Christ returns and thinks to himself, "I can't wait for that day to come because I will put on my new resurrection body like I put on an overcoat."

Answer # 2: It is the end of our groaning.

We groan because of a job we hate. We groan because of unfulfilled dreams. We groan because our bodies break down. We groan because our marriages break up. We groan because our children go astray. We groan because our friends disappoint us.

We groan because we live in a fallen, mixed-up, messed-up, broken-down world, and we ourselves are broken down. So we look for a better day and a better place, and we dream of a better world where there is …

No more cancer.
No more abuse.
No more hatred.
No more hurricanes.
No more crime.
No more sadness.
No more night.
No more sickness.
No more death.

Answer # 3: It removes our deepest fears.

Among all the fears associated with death, one of the greatest must be that we will die alone and forgotten. As sad as death seems, how much worse it must be to die in some distant place with no one around to give you comfort. How blessed we are if we can die with our loved ones gathered by our side. Often that is not possible because death comes unbidden to our door. We may end up dying in some lonely place despite our best plans.

What is the current condition of believers who die before Jesus returns? *The clearest thing we can say is that they are "with Christ" and "with the Lord" in heaven.* Paul says as much in verses 6–8. We don't have to worry about our loved ones who died in Christ. They have passed into the presence of the Lord Jesus himself. That, I think, is all we can know for certain, but it is enough. Paul says clearly that the dead in Christ will rise first when Christ returns (1 Thessalonians 4:13–18). That's the moment when those who die in Christ receive their resurrection bodies. Between now and then it is enough and more than enough to know they are "with the Lord" and will be with him forever.

When we die, we will not die alone because we will be with Jesus forever. If we should live to see Christ return, we will receive our resurrection body at that very moment. Either way, we have a hope that death cannot shake.

One question remains. Paul, how can you be so sure?

The Guarantee of the Resurrection Body

"Now it is God who has made us for this very purpose and has given us the Spirit as a deposit, guaranteeing what is to come" (v. 5).

Sometimes we look at the world around us and wonder, "Is that all there is?" To which Paul answers a resounding, "No!" We were made for something better than the sadness we see in this world.

We will have a new body—not the same as before.
We will have a new body—not just renovated or reconstructed.
We will have a new body—but our identity will not change.

We are made for a new life and a new body and a new existence with the Lord. God himself has made us for this very purpose. Our future depends on the eternal purpose of God who called us to be his children. *We are saved by an eternal love that will not let us go.* Not even death can separate us from the love of God in Christ Jesus our Lord.

Here, then, is a hopeful thought for anyone who has buried a loved one who died in the Lord. How do we know we will see them again? *The answer is, it all depends on where we look.* You can go to a cemetery, take a lawn chair with you, and sit there with some sweet tea and a ham sandwich. Go and wait as long as you want. You'll see lots of death because that's what cemeteries are all about. Lots of people being buried; not many being raised from the dead. In fact, the last resurrection took place 2,000 years ago.

So how do we know there is a coming day of resurrection? There are two solid answers to that question.

Answer # 1: He raised his own Son.

The first answer is that God raised his own Son from the dead. *This is the objective ground of our faith in the coming day of resurrection.* If God would not leave his Son in the grave, he will not abandon those who trusted in his Son. Death cannot win in the end because our Lord conquered the grave.

Answer # 2: He gave us the Spirit as a sacred deposit.

Paul mentions the second answer in verse 5. God gave us the Spirit as a "deposit." Some translations say "down payment" or "earnest." When you buy a house, you put down a sum of money called "earnest money." It's a small amount that legally binds you to pay the full amount later. That's what God has done through his Holy Spirit. The Spirit who indwells us is God's "down payment" on our future resurrection.

God signed on the dotted line and said, "I will raise from the dead all who have trusted in my Son." Then he made the down payment through the gift of the Holy Spirit.

It's as good as done.

It's going to happen.

You can take it to the bank.

What should this truth do for us today? *It changes the way we look at death.* We have it all wrong. We think we're going from the land of the living to the land of the dying. But that is not true. We're going from the land of the dying to the land of the living.

By the way, what is required for a resurrection? *You've got to die first!* No death, no resurrection. Unless the Lord comes very soon (I think he may, and I hope he does), that will be the way most of us will end our earthly journey.

Someway, somehow, someday we'll die. Whoever is around at that moment will take us to the mortuary where the undertaker will do what he does to prepare us for our burial. We'll be dressed up and cleaned up and made up to look semi-natural, but we'll still be dead. Then they will take us in for the funeral service where someone will say some (hopefully) nice words, people will remark on how they miss us, they will sing a bit, say some prayers, and then the box will close, and we'll be placed in the ground.

I say that not to alarm anyone, but to state the simple fact that we're all going to do some "box time" eventually. The man who wrote this uplifting passage in 2 Corinthians 5 returned to the dust of the earth a few years later. Every Christian who has ever lived has died eventually. So far, that's the report from the cemetery.

But, thank God, it's not the last word. If you have a loved one who died in Christ, you should go out to the grave and have a little talk. Maybe it's your grandfather who loved the Lord and is now buried in the grave. Just go out there and say this with confidence, "Grandpa, I miss you, and I'm glad you are with the Lord right now. But I want you to know God is not finished with you yet. He's got some more work to do."

Then maybe you can read this passage out loud just to remind yourself of what Christians really believe.

Bright and Cloudless Morning

In early 2009 we buried my dear friend John Sergey who was over 90 years old. It was my privilege to speak at his funeral and again at his graveside service. When I stood by the casket, I reminded the folks that besides being a mighty preacher of the gospel, John also loved to play and sing gospel songs. I quoted a verse from one of his favorite songs:

> On that bright and cloudless morning when the
> dead in Christ shall rise,
> And the glory of his resurrection share;
> When his chosen ones shall gather to their home
> beyond the skies,
> And the roll is called up yonder, I'll be there.

That's our ultimate hope. We're not looking for some hazy view of heaven where we float around on clouds all day. We're looking and waiting and longing for that "bright and cloudless morning" when the Lord returns and the dead in Christ shall rise.

It's going to happen.
You can bet your life on it.
God has promised it.

When Christ saves you, he saves all of you. Every part of you is saved and every part of you will be delivered from sin. It is not *soul* salvation that we believe in but *whole* salvation. The resurrection of the body is the final step in our salvation:

Step #1: We are saved from the *penalty* of sin.
Step #2: We are saved from the *power* of sin.
Step #3: We are saved from the *presence* of sin.

I ran across a beautiful phrase from the *Pulpit Commentary* that lifts my heart every time I read it. *There will be "victory on the last battlefield.*" Life is a series of battles for all of us, and we all "take it on the chin" sooner or later. But in the last battle, the struggle with death, there is victory for the children of God.

"Death, be not proud," wrote John Donne. *God will not let death win.* Henry Wadsworth Longfellow expressed the same truth in his poem "God's Acre." Here are the first and last stanzas:

> I like that ancient Saxon phrase, which calls
> The burial-ground God's-Acre! It is just;
> It consecrates each grave within its walls,
> And breathes a benison o'er the sleeping dust.
>
> With thy rude ploughshare, Death, turn up the sod,
> And spread the furrow for the seed we sow;
> This is the field and Acre of our God,
> This is the place where human harvests grow.

What an image that is: "the place where human harvests grow." Go to any graveyard where Christians are buried and there you will find "God's Acre." Take off your shoes. It is holy ground. *Human harvests are growing there.* I close with the words of the Puritan writer Thomas Watson: "We are more sure to arise out of our graves than out of our beds. Oh! How precious is the dust of a believer!"

Death will not have the last word for Jesus has conquered the grave. Because he rose, we too shall rise. In that faith we take courage to live for Christ with reckless abandon because death is not the end of our story.

13

THE CHOICE WE MUST MAKE

Sometimes we have more questions than answers.

I still remember the week when I buried two 42-year-old men who had died of cancer. Later I spoke a funeral service for a premature baby who was born three months early and died after two days. As I left that room in the funeral home, I went across the hall to comfort a wife whose husband had dropped dead while he was walking into the hospital.

As the years pass, it doesn't get any easier. And the questions remain. I received a message from one of our missionaries. A colleague was terribly injured in an automobile accident. Although he lived for a week, he died suddenly in the middle of the night. With total honesty the missionary bared his soul.

> My heart is in shock. Why, God? My friend and his wife gave up their current professions to serve God as youth pastor missionaries. He is especially built for being a youth pastor. God designed him with such passion in life. And more than that, passion toward

people. And more than that, passion toward God. He has constantly been a source of encouragement. Why, God? I really don't understand. I really don't even pretend to understand. I have so many questions. God, why him? And why now? After such an encouraging come-back for a whole week! God is so weird. I am not saying bad, but weird. I do not understand him.

Why? Why now? Why this? How could God do such a thing?

It is easier to ask the questions than to answer them. And any answer will seem pitifully inadequate, especially to the one suffering such a loss. But the missionary is also a Christian, and he provided part of his own answer. It was raining hard when he heard the news of his colleague's death. The thought occurred to him that it only takes a few degrees difference in temperature to change rain into snow. Rain, he said, speaks of death, depression, and sorrow, while snow speaks of freshness, life, and heaven. Then he drew this conclusion:

> Just a few degrees change. In water the change is so very small. The change from the earthly plane to the spiritual seems so very great … at least from the earthly viewpoint. My friend being in heaven seems so crystal clear. Clear to what I do not know, but it seems so good. I still have a whole lot of "why?" questions for God. And at times I ask them out of anger. But at the same time, they don't seem as significant in light of seeing a vivid picture of him enjoying heaven and God our Father delighting in him.

In every great moment of crisis, we all have a choice to make. Either we will choose to believe in God, or we won't. More specifically, we will choose to believe God is good, or we won't. In the times of pain and loss, that choice must be made by faith, not because of what has happened, but often in spite of it.

I cannot prove to you God is good any more than I can prove the existence of heaven or that Jesus Christ is the Son of God. I can simply tell you what the Bible says and what the people of God have discovered across the centuries.

Choosing to believe God is good will not exempt you from sorrow and suffering, nor will it guarantee you an easy road to follow. But it will put a firm foundation beneath your feet as you journey from earth to heaven. As I close this book, I am drawn again to the words of A. J. Gossip, who said to those who wondered why he still believed in God after his wife's tragic death: "You people in the sunshine may believe the faith, but we in the shadow must believe it. We have nothing else."

I've thought a lot about that in the last few months. Death comes to all of us sooner or later, and we will all spend time in the school of suffering. Sometimes the road does indeed become very steep and the way very dark. But we have a wonderful God.

If you believe that, you can face things that would destroy most people. Indeed, if you believe that, you can face your own death with confidence and courage.

One final word from Pastor Gossip. "I don't think you need to be afraid of life." There is a reason the Bible calls him the God of all comfort. It is in his very nature to comfort his people in all their afflictions. With that confidence we can go forward one step at a time, walking into the future without fear, taking all that life has to offer—the good and the bad together, even when some questions remain unanswered.

He is the God of all comfort. Fear not and keep believing in him.

ABOUT THE AUTHOR

Dr. Ray Pritchard (D.Min., Talbot School of Theology; graduate of Tennessee Temple University and Dallas Theological Seminary) serves as president of Keep Believing Ministries. For 26 years he pastored churches in Los Angeles, Dallas and Chicago. His span of experience—from ministering overseas, to guest-lecturing, to co-hosting *Today's Issues* on American Family Radio—provides a unique supply of knowledge and insight.

Dr. Pritchard has authored 31 books, including *An Anchor for the Soul*, *Stealth Attack*, *The Healing Power of Forgiveness*, *Credo: Believing in Something to Die For*, *In the Shadow of the Cross*, and *Why Did This Happen to Me?*

Dr. Pritchard has been married to his wife, Marlene, for 44 years. Their three sons are married, and they have eight grandchildren.

SPECIAL NOTE

You can follow the author on social media:

Facebook: https://www.facebook.com/raypritchard
Twitter: https://twitter.com/raypritchard

If you would like to contact the author, you can reach him in the following ways:

By letter:
Ray Pritchard
P. O. Box 257
Elmhurst, IL 60126

By email: ray@keepbelieving.com
Via the internet: www.keepbelieving.com